HOW TO MAKE KNIVES

Richard W. Barney
Robert W. Loveless

Other Publications by Krause Publications, Inc.

Blade Magazine

EDGES, the Newspaper of Knives

Pocketknives Repair: A Cutler's Manual

How To Make Folding Knives

IBCA Price Guide To Antique Knives

Collin's Bowies & Machetes 1845-1965

Krause Publications, Inc.   700 E. State Street, Iola, WI   54990

Phone (715) 445-2214   FAX (715) 445-4087

Managing Editor: Wallace Beinfeld
Senior Technical Editor: A. G. Russell
Technical Editors: Michael Collins
Corbet Sigman
Jim Small
Buster Warenski
Designer: L. S. Beinfeld

On the Cover
A subhilt fighter crafted by co-author
R. W. Loveless and Steve
Johnson. Photographed by Jim
Weyer of Toledo, Ohio, from
the book of knife photography,
"Knives: Points of Interest."

Warning: Neither the authors nor Krause Publications assume any responsibility, directly or indirectly, for the safety of readers attempting to make their own knives following instructions in this book. Knifemaking should be approached with caution and safety in mind. Those inexperienced in the use of power tools such as grinders and buffers should take extra-special precautions in their use. As any veteran knifemaker can tell you, knifemaking can be very hazardous to your health. Be careful.

krause publications
An Imprint of F+W Publications

700 East State Street • Iola, WI 54990-0001
715-445-2214 • 888-457-2873
www.krausebooks.com

ISBN 13: 978-0-87341-389-3
ISBN 10: 0-87341-389-X

Printed in the United States of America

I have been privileged to watch the handmade knife industry grow from five makers producing knives for sale and perhaps five dozen making them as a hobby, to well over one hundred makers offering their wares to the public, and several thousand enjoying knifemaking as a most rewarding hobby. I believe that the real growth has not yet begun in the field of the hobbyist who wants to make knives for his own pleasure and use.

You are reading this because you are interested in handmade knives. Either you want to make them or you want to know what kind of work goes into a fine knife. I believe that you may have come to the right place. In this book, two of the finest knifemakers in history will take you into their shops and show you, step by step, just how they make their knives. In addition, other great makers have added their tips on how they make fine knives.

Since you may be new to handmade knives, I will give you some background on two of these men.

Robert W. Loveless has been, for the past seven years, widely acknowledged as the premier maker of hunting and combat knives. There is no question that Loveless has had more influence on the design of modern handmade knives than anyone else.

I don't think there is any better place to learn the stock removal method of knifemaking than in Bob Loveless' shop, so step in and look over his shoulder.

William F. Moran is one of that rare class of knifemakers, "The Knifesmith." He forges every blade. Bill has been forging knives for well over twenty-five years and a few years ago redeveloped the hand-forged Damascus blade. This is an enormous accomplishment and would be enough to establish his fame, even if he had not been making fine hunting knives for many, many years.

If you want to make authentic period pieces in the original way, follow Bill into his shop and he will show you the tools and methods you should use.

The third section of this book shows Richard W. Barney using shop tools and reasonably priced hand tools to show that he, too, is an accomplished knifemaker. Here he shows how to do first class work with a modest amount of power and a few simple hand tools. If you actually want to make a knife, this is the way to start.

In addition to collaborating with Robert W. Loveless in the writing of the three major sections of this book, Richard W. Barney has traveled the United States, visiting the shops of Buster Warenski, Jim Small, Corbet Sigman, and Michael Collins, and researching additional techniques valuable to a new knifemaker. As a result, you will find here the work of the cream of today's makers.

I hope that you enjoy this book and your involvement with handmade knives as much as I have enjoyed being in the knife business these past years.

A. G. Russell
Springdale, Arkansas
Spring 1977

Because we have written this book as a textbook for readers who intend to buy tools and materials and then go to work, the text has been put into a certain order. First of all, we suggest you read the section concerning safety. Knifemaking is hazardous, and you must be aware of the potential problems and the risks of carelessness.

Next, we have fully described the two major ways of making knives, as practiced by two full-time knifemakers. Both the forging and the stock removal methods are covered, and we urge a careful study of this material before you begin your own work.

Pay particular attention to the photographs. We have used the pictures to show you the many steps involved; they are explicit and detailed.

We have discussed both the tools and the materials of knifemaking very carefully, in the hope that this part of the book will be most useful to the beginning worker. Where costs are mentioned, they are accurate as of the date of this publication; bear in mind that the prices listed will increase, possibly by as much as ten percent each year. Where we have shown you ways to save money we know such ideas work, because we have tried them ourselves.

Finally, we have included a complete listing of the equipment and materials sources known to us. These sources have established their reliability in their relationships with knifemakers now working, and every effort has been made to insure that you will be able to obtain your requirements from the companies listed.

Inevitably, some questions will not have been answered; some of the answers may come from you. We hope that as you develop your own methods, you will bear in mind that many thousands of individual men, working down through the ages, have freely shared their knowledge and techniques with others, and that you, too, will want to pass on your own ideas. Making knives is interesting, even fascinating, and we are convinced that the very finest knives are ahead of us, yet to be made. We invite you to contribute to succeeding editions, by addressing your comments to the publisher.

Richard W. Barney and Robert W. Loveless
Riverside, California, Spring 1977

SECTION I
ABOUT KNIFEMAKING

A HISTORY OF HANDMADE KNIVES

Probably, if we knew the truth of things, we would find that at least as many knives have been made by individual men, working alone, down through history, as have been made by all the factories now working. Consider the earliest knives we know of: stone knives, made when men were just beginning to learn how to make tools. Then, later, flint knives were probably made by a single man of the tribe who had learned to specialize and concentrate his labor. Next, the use of bronze was learned, and knives were made of it. Finally, and only recently in the story of man, iron and steel knives were made, crudely at first, but by the time of the birth of Christ, they were refined and sophisticated, and are worthy even now of serious study by both concerned archaeologists and modern collectors.

But this history will begin in relatively recent times, to cover the achievements of certain men who worked well, and lit the way for those who would follow; men like Scagle, Ruana, Randall, and the others who came later. We will look briefly at what we Americans, coming here mostly from Europe, brought with us from the old country, because even now we have not completely abandoned that early heritage.

We had not hunted much in Europe, where hunting rights belonged only to the upper classes. We were artisans, farmers, religious dissenters; some of us were convicts, banished forever to a new and untamed land. Soon a few of us left the settlements and went west from the eastern seaboard into the woods, acquiring new experiences, discovering new needs, and ways to meet them. The western frontier in those early days was the Pennsylvania and Ohio and Kentucky country, and each successive movement brought us into conflict with red men, tribal Indians who were far more at home in that country than the early white travelers. But we had gunpowder and firearms, and even then, fine knives, which were the very first of the white man's goods to be traded, bartered for hunting and trapping rights, and just a little later, farming areas. And by then, the English cutlers had discovered the frontier market, making and selling the so-called "trade knives" to the colonies where such blades soon became a working currency in the commerce between red and white men.

From the late seventeenth century until the middle years of the nineteenth, when white men dominated most of the useful lands of the North American continent, the trade knives were bartered often with barrels of trade whiskey. Each passing decade saw the tribal confederations lose more power, for there was, indeed, no end to these Ango-Saxon conquerors.

The way west was traveled by the mountain men, who were seeking riches in the form of beaver pelts, and who soon came to be hired hands of the major fur companies. These men had their own knives even then, in the early decades of the nineteenth century, heavy knives used for rough work, and some fine, carefully sharpened smaller blades, kept in their "possibles" bag and used for skinning, repairing clothes, and even field surgery. The prairie and mountain red men saw these knives and preferred them above all other trade goods. Indeed, it was the knives and guns of the newcomers which first gave certain far-seeing Indian leaders concern about the invasion of the whites.

After the Civil War, American military men assigned to western posts soon realized what had to be done to whip the Plains Indians: kill the buffalo! Ordinary citizens were flooding west, looking for new land. A veteran of the recent bitter conflict had little sympathy for the Indians' way of life; he wanted land. His government had passed legislation and land was to be his bonus for faithful service on the Union side.

Confederate veterans, knowing they would get short rations indeed from the victors, packed their horses and goods and soon were on the move. Some of them tried trapping, but that way of life was mostly gone by 1865. Others went to Texas and into the cattle business. Still others joined the western Army, where a few had served before the war.

All these men, both Union and Confederate veterans and others who were seeking new chances, moved west, across the "Big Muddy." They found mile after mile of flatland and grassland, seemingly capable of growing anything, and the fight was on in earnest; conquer the Plains tribes, plant crops and settle the vast country, expand the great American nation, make progress! Go all the way to the mighty Pacific, Americans; there's room enough for all!

And indeed there was, then. But first, the Indians. And the answer was simple, for anyone who knew the Plains tribes; eliminate their commissary, the vast buffalo herds. And so the buffalo hunters came, by the thousands. It was a way to make good money, and also serve the cause of the country. Men who had only a few years before used their Bowie knives (mostly made by English cutlers) in war, now came to use the hide-skinning knives of the John Russell Company, and Lamson and Goodnow, and the other Connecticut Valley cutleries, and soon the hide wagons were moving into Omaha by the hundreds, and into other shipping points, where hundreds of thousands of pounds of green hide were on the way to tanneries. Buffalo skinning knives are still made today by the same company that made them then, Russell-Hyde, and by others. The buffalo are long gone, but the knives are still used where beef cows are converted to choice cuts of meat for millions of Americans.

In the Louisiana-Texas country, the legendary James Bowie became a hero to the young country in the early decades of the "Century of Expansion." He moved in land speculation and traded in slaves, dealt with Lafitte, the pirate, and Juan Veramendi, the Mexican Governor of Texas, made friends and enemies along the early southwestern frontier. He carved a record with his knife (and we suspect it was several knives, rather than a single "Iron Mistress," at least in his early years) that stands to this day. Bowie pioneered, worked and fought in man-to-man combat for little more than a decade, from the mid 1820s until his death at the Alamo in 1836. Yet the power of the Bowie legend even today governs the shapes of modern knives.

No man interested in the history of knives in America can ignore Jim Bowie and his story. Think of his fight with Major Norris Wright on the Sand Bar above Natchez, his adventures up and down the Trace, his final settling in Texas (then under Mexican administration), his taste of tragedy in losing his wife and children to illness while absent from home on business, his later involvement in the cause of Texas freedom, and finally his death, if the popular version be true, at the hand of the Alamo assault forces while down with a broken hip.

Truly a star-crossed man, a man among men, Bowie's story was told, first by his contemporaries, and then by journalists in the eastern papers. All along the Great River road, from St. Louis to Natchez to New Orleans, the schools of arms came to teach the art of the fighting knife along with the sword cane, and every man of the times owned and carried his Bowie knife. Within a decade after his death, at a time when every American freely carried arms, state legislatures passed laws prohibiting the use of the Bowie knife, and even the carrying of it. Still it was carried, and worn, and used across the west to the far California country. By the beginning of the Civil War it was probably the best-known knife in America. Today, the name "Bowie Knife" applies to most any large knife from 6 to 10 inches in blade length, with the clipped point that is so typical of the design. As with any legend, the Bowie Knife has come to be about whatever the maker says it is and even the authorities do not exactly agree on what the original knife looked like.

All during the Bowie Knife years, Americans were farming, working, hunting, and taking care of business. We were also developing our own unique knives. Blacksmiths in cities, small towns, and in the small frontier settlements tried their hand at making knives. The small cutlers' shops of New England, located along rivers and streams that furnished water power to run the forges and grinding wheels, were growing too. By the time of the Civil War they had developed into a full-fledged cutlery industry. No longer dependent on English steel, the American cutlery companies were supplying the country completely by the late decades of the nineteenth century. They were also exporting knives back to the Europeans, and to new markets around the world.

Cutlery has always been, from the earliest days, an extremely competitive business, subject to the varying conditions of the American economy. In the years following the Civil War, U.S. cutlery companies became fewer and larger; product lines were simplified and standardized and quality was, if not ignored, certainly relegated to second or even third place in the race to survive the depressions of the late nineteenth century and the hectic early years of the twentieth.

By World War I, the country was settled. Cutlery was no longer the important business it had been fifty years earlier. In the Connecticut Valley towns and elsewhere the race was on to cut costs and develop ways to mass-produce cheap knives; that was what the trade seemed to want and the companies aimed to provide it. After the war, and into the 1920s, a few shops set up but the Great Depression came to grip the country by the throat, and by 1931 or 1932 few men cared much about fine knives; we had other things to think about. Besides, who needed really good knives anyway? The crying need all over the world was for food, enough to eat; and employment, getting people back on their feet. their feet.

(1A) These unusual hunting knives with one folding blade, were a specialty of William Scagel. Circa: Mid 1930s. Photo by Scagel himself, now in Tru-Bal collection.
(Courtesy H. K. McEvoy)

(1B) Typical Scagel knives of the 1930-1940 period. Photo taken by Scagel himself.
(Courtesy H. K. McEvoy)

5

Yet even then, a few men were working, in their own small shops, to make fine individual handmade knives for customers who would settle for nothing less. One of these was a man named Scagel, working in Michigan. Very much his own man, Bill Scagel made hundreds of knives, each of them one at a time, and rarely any two exactly alike. Working with machinery and equipment he had designed and made himself, deliberately locating off the beaten track where he wouldn't be bothered, Bill Scagel labored on work he must have loved, for he did it well and truly, with devotion and respect, until his death at an advanced age in 1963.

(2) Collection of Scagel knives in the Randall Made Knives "Museum". (Courtesy Randall Made Knives)

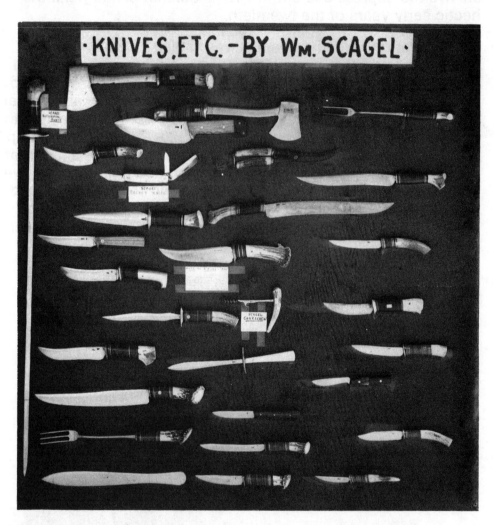

·KNIVES, ETC. – BY WM. SCAGEL·

And it was in 1936 that another man, one W.D. Randall, staying at his summer home in Michigan, came upon a Scagel knife being used to scrape the bottom of a boat. Randall recognized a fine knife, made a deal for it, and took it home. Then, as has been know to happen with other men a time or two, Bo Randall fell in love with that Scagel knife. He became obsessed with Scagel's knife, so much so that he decided to make knives himself. He visited Scagel, received encouragment, went back home to Orlando, Florida, and went to work.

6

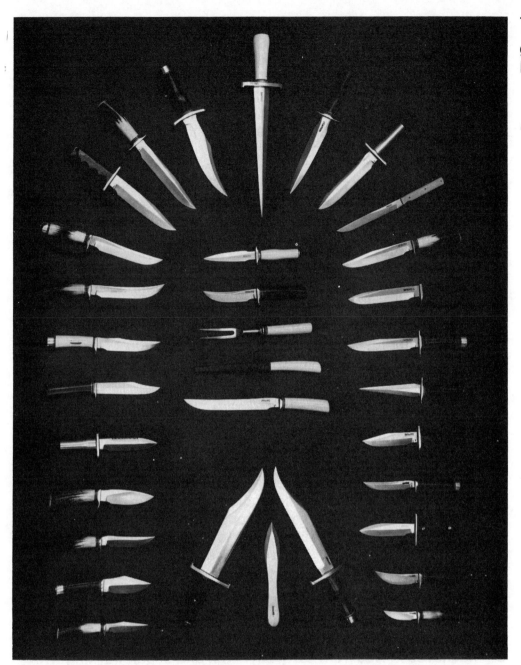

(3) A representative group of Randall Made Knives.

If Bill Scagel was a legend known only to a few, Bo Randall's career as a working knifemaker, beginning in the late 1930s, ultimately brought him worldwide fame, as he single-handedly kept the tradition of high quality handmade knives alive for the next three decades. The Randall shop today continues working, inspiring other men to try their hand at fine knifemaking.

During the early 1950s, readers of the *American Rifleman* magazine often saw small, one-inch deep, one-column wide advertisements for three working knifemakers. One of these was Bo Randall; the other two were Rudy Ruana, working in Bonner, Montana, and Harry Morseth, working out of Morseth Sports Equipment Company, in Washington state.

Ruana's knives were low-priced, somewhat crude by comparison with other such work, but strong and honestly made. The story goes that Ruana had been in Pershing's column in the Mexican campaign after Pancho Villa, taking care of the farrier's duties, and that sometime later, he had settled in Montana and turned his hand to other things in the blacksmithing line, finally settling into making knives out of automotive spring steel stock for local customers. Soon Ruana knives had made their mark, and may be found today, especially in the northwestern hunting country, working away in the hands of outdoorsmen who know a good thing when they have it. On a fall hunt in Montana in 1961, your author tried to buy a Ruana away from the guide who was using it, only to be bluntly told, "Git yer own, I'm busy".

Harry Morseth imported his stock from Brusletto, in Norway, ground his blades finely, and mounted his own handles on them. Those blades were thin, compared to other knives, about 1/8 of an inch thick, and made up of a center core layer of high-carbon steel, faced with outer layers of softer iron, and you couldn't hardly break them! Harry's original knives were neat, light, working knives, with fine edge-holding, and again, highly valued by their owners. With the death of Harry Morseth, a grandson, Steve, took over the shop, tried to run things for a few years, and finally the shop was sold to A.G. Russell, of Springdale, Arkansas, who still offers Morseth laminated blades from imported stock.

One day in 1954, a man walked into Abercrombie & Fitch, the famous New York City sporting goods store, to buy a Randall knife. Told he would have to wait for months, he left, made up a knife of his own, took it back to the store and became a working knifemaker in pretty short order. That man was R.W. Loveless, who was working on a Sun Oil Company tanker in New York harbor at the time. Since then he has made quite a few knives at his shop in Riverside, California.

Or consider another man written about in this book, Bill Moran. Bill had loved knives from early boyhood, and began working with his forge on the farm in Lime Kiln, Maryland, while still a schoolboy. By the mid 1950s, his reputation had begun to grow, and today he is recognized as the preeminent forging knifemaker in the country.

And then there is the Buck family. Buck knives were made by H. H. Buck right after World War II, and as demand for his knives grew, son Al went to work in the shop. Today, the Buck Knife Company employs several hundred people making their line of outdoor knives in El Cajon, California.

Knifemaking by individual men suddenly began to come alive in the early 1970s. The Knifemakers Guild was established in 1970 and by 1974 had dozens of members. Today, such well-known names as D.E. Henry, H.H. Frank, Harvey Draper, George Herron, T.M. Dowell, Jess Horn, and dozens of others are talked about when knife lovers get together.

What of tomorrow? Will some reader of this book become inspired to go to work, learn the techniques offered, develop even better ones of his own and go on to create a place for himself in the world of knifemaking? We most certainly hope so; the making of fine knives is a dynamic thing, and none of us can see the end of it. The future does not belong only to armies and governments and great powers: individual men can still strive for mighty goals, if they will but try.

SAFETY STARTS WITH YOUR STATE OF MIND

Knifemaking can be compared to high-speed driving on the freeway. Make one mistake, get absent-minded for just one moment, and you may be injured so badly you will be unable to work for weeks. So pay strict attention as you work, and always keep in mind the consequences of carelessness.

Hand and eye injuries are the most common. When you realize how important your hands and eyes are, think for a minute of having to live your daily life without either. Yet by using the proper protection, and being sensible, you can work confidently.

(1) Protect your eyes. Safety glasses are a MUST.

The primary prevention for eye injuries is eye protection, some form of goggles or eyeshield. Note that well, and never pick up a tool without having your eyes covered. Even when doing light bench work, such as filing, be sure to wear your safety glasses (1). If you wear prescription glasses, have your optometrist fit you with prescription safety glasses before doing anything in your shop.

(2) A face shield will provide total eye protection.

When using a belt grinder, to grind bevels for instance, the best safety glasses are not good enough! Buy and wear a full face shield, and be sure it's adjusted to your head size (2). Be especially careful when working with any power equipment, such as the belt grinder, the drill press, and the buffing heads mounted on the polishing lathe. All these tools work fast, under power, and minute chips of material often are propelled through the air with force enough to puncture the eyeball.

It can't be said too strongly: *cover your eyes!* Never, under any circumstances, no matter how much of a hurry you are in, never work without covering your eyes. And if you think we are being too fussy, ask yourself this: how much would you sell your eyes for? Just how much money would you take to give up being able to see what goes on around you? We don't think there *is* that much money.

Stop and think for a moment about why you bought this book. Picture in your mind just what a knife is. It's a cutting tool, isn't it? Now consider how soft your skin is, and how hard and sharp a knife is, and you'll begin to understand the danger. And don't think for even a second that only a hardened and sharpened knife can cut you; any piece of steel being worked up that has a burr on some edge of it can hurt you, badly.

Nor is steel the only danger. Steel chips in the eye can be removed by a surgeon with a small magnet, but that won't help you if you've caught a brass or aluminum chip!

(3)Be careful. That bandsaw can hurt you.

Be especially careful when using the belt grinder on any material during any kind of powered operation. Watch yourself when using the powered bandsaw, even for low-speed steel sawing, and be extra careful when using high blade speeds to cut handle materials, for instance (3). That bandsaw, by the way, is probably the single most hazardous tool in any small shop; one single action of carelessness and you are going to have part of a finger lost, at least.

(4) The push stick will save fingers.

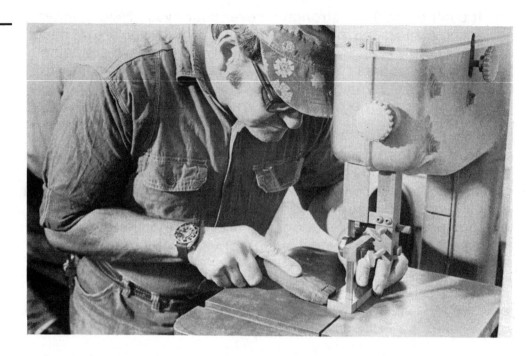

Use a push stick for your early work (4) until you have become thoroughly familiar with how this tool works, and be sure to change the blade as soon as it gets dull, so that you don't get bitten at the end of a cut because you've been pushing too hard to be able to stop quickly as the blade breaks free (5). And don't try to work with the bandsaw if someone is nearby carrying on a conversation with you.

(5) Keep from pushing too hard as the blade breaks free.

In fact, be careful about being distracted by anything or anyone. Being surprised when making a roughing cut on the grinder by someone coming into the shop can distract you just as you are moving your hand toward the sharp edge of the 60 grit belt and you'll end up with a very painful cut. The grinding belt both cuts and burns as it tears the skin, and these cuts sometimes take forever to heal. If your wife comes into the shop to ask about supper, shut down the machine, right there and then. Even though you are trying to get that bevel finished before supper, stop the machine! Trying to handle a knife and fork with a badly cut hand takes an awful lot of pleasure out of your food, friend.

(6) The WRONG way to cut.

Going to cut off a length of stock clamped in a vise with a hacksaw? Well, there's a right way, and a wrong way, and if you use the wrong way (6), chances are your hand is going to get nicked or cut. If you are right-handed, work on the right side of the vise (7), and ease up the cutting pressure just as you get almost through the cut so you don't slam your closed fist into its ragged edge (8).

(7) The RIGHT way, for a right-hander.

(8)Ease up at the end of the cut.

Are you about ready to mark a hole location with your center punch and hammer? Take a minute to check the head of the punch; if it's mushroomed, dress it off on the grinder before using it so the hammer won't drive a chip from the head of the punch into your eye.

Trying to finish off your newest skinner to show your hunting partner later in the evening when he comes over? Stop right there! NOTHING CAN HURT YOU AS MUCH AS TRYING TO GO TOO FAST. Learn that rule, and live by it. Take your time. Work carefully, knowing in advance what the next step is. Have your tools ready, fresh blade in the hacksaw, etc., and work at a slow and steady planned pace. **Safety always starts with your state of mind.**

Every knifemaker, sooner or later, mounts a soft cotton buffing wheel on a buffer and gets into the job of polishing the blade. And every knifemaker, sooner or later, has that blade snatched out of his hands by the action of the buffing wheel. If you're lucky the blade slams into the floor behind the buffer. But if you aren't lucky it can end up sticking out of your own leg, and you are out of business for some time. Look at the picture series showing the various surfaces being polished. Note that we go with the blades away from the edges, and not toward them. This is important, and here's why: the blade is usually almost finished at this point, needing only sharpening of the hone to be done. The point is sharp and very much ready to bite if you get careless. So here is a tip: practice on a piece of 1-inch diameter round bar stock and get to know how the buffing action works. You will acquire the ability to handle the buffing wheel; your hands will get stronger and steadier and you'll lose your fear of things as you become familiar with the tool. Don't use too much pressure on the buffer; if the work is not coming up, you may not be using enough compound, so coat the wheel again with the rouge stick (9). Just as with any other power tool, learn how it works before trying to do fancy work with it.

(9)The correct amount of compound will help at the buffer.

(10)Clamp up for safety.

Ready to drill holes on the drill press? Clamp up the job so that the work won't jerk out of your hand as the drill breaks through (10). Later on you'll learn how to hold a 1/8-inch drill, but no man can safely hold a 1/2-inch drill, cutting through soft steel. Yes, we realize that many workers do exactly that, but don't learn such bad habits. A couple of rules about drill press work: the bigger the drill, the more force it has to hurt you. And the smaller the part, the harder it is to hold on to. So when you are drilling out the guard holes, clamp up the part in a drill press vise and clamp that to the table. And whatever else you do, DO NOT reach out to grab the spiral chips and get them out of the way. Those chips are like razors, and work the same way.

The Big Fellow sure didn't design us human beings with a view to being knifemakers. If He had, we'd come equipped with respirators already in place. Because grinding steel and brass and staghorn and Micarta, etc., releases all kinds of junk into the air around the grinder. And short of wearing a bottle of breathing oxygen, you have to breathe that air. We call it air, but it's loaded with all kinds of funny stuff, stuff that you'll drag into your lungs if you forget, just for a minute, to put on your respirator. Sure, the heavier chips and metal particles will fall quickly to the floor, but the light stuff will stay suspended in the air for hours, and none of it is good for your lungs.

(11)Wear your respirator.

A respirator (11) will catch most of this stuff, but nobody knows just what effect the fine dust of some of the African hardwood handle materials will do to human lungs over a period of several years. What we do know, however, is that some knifemakers become violently ill very quickly when grinding this material. The stuff called Micarta is, in fact, layers of fabric laminated in a phenolic resin: grinding a Micarta-handled knife releases the strong odor of phenol, and we doubt very much if your family doctor would feel happy about that.

Hand and eye injuries are quickly obvious, but lung damage is not. You can't see it, and a momentary shortness of breath is often blamed on the latest head cold. Don't you believe it. VENTILATE your shop. Install some kind of blower to exhaust the bad air outside the grinding and buffing area. Yes, buffing: it's just as bad as grinding. The various buffing compounds are usually made up of very fine, powdery, abrasive particles, suspended in a wax or stiff grease base. Coated on the buffing wheel, they actually burn off into the air. You may not notice it, but you'll smell it. And if you can smell it, it's going to hurt you over the long haul.

WEAR A RESPIRATOR. VENTILATE YOUR WORK AREA. If you don't do these things you will have nobody to blame but yourself if, several years from now, you find yourself so short of breath that you can no longer live a normal life. Because, you see, nobody else can make you work safely. Your wife may care what happens to you, but few others will. It is completely up to you, alone, and you alone will have to acquire the habit of working safely. You'll have to learn to plan your work so that you are not ever rushed and in a hurry. You'll have to light your shop so that you aren't fumbling for a certain tool, or stumbling over something as you move around. If you are going to forge steel, you will have to learn to cope with hot scale flying through the air and how to handle your forging fire safely. You'll have to plan and buy your own First Aid Kit, provided with dressings, bandages, and antiseptics, so that when you do get a small cut you can take care of it promptly, instead of ignoring it.

If the label on the solder says to work in a well-ventilated place, you ignore that warning at your own peril. Solders and fluxes often have poisonous substances in them, and can hurt you quickly if you get careless. Know where your machine switches are: have the "OFF" switch fixed in your mind so you don't have to grope for it. Wear safety shoes when handling heavy work. (A Bowie knife blade can cripple you if it lands hard enough on the arch of your foot.) Learn, quickly, that any sharp-edged piece of steel can cut you and wear work gloves whenever you can, but not when using power equipment like the drill press. When working there, take off your wedding ring and even your wrist watch and roll up your sleeves, out of the way. Watch your fingers when you turn on the bandsaw. Be aware of your own posture at the workbench; stand clear and be able to move quickly.

Don't let the blade get hot when grinding. You can't grip that hot steel firmly, and that's when you are going to lose it, maybe into your leg. Handle hot solder carefully; it splashes just like water, but burns like liquid fire. Keep your tools in good shape, ready for work and in their proper place, always. And keep your own head in proper condition, too. If you've had a beef with the woman in your life, stay out of the knife shop for an evening; take her out to dinner, maybe.

And if you are the kind of person who is always having small accidents, forget all this; take up playing chess, or stamp collecting, because knifemaking is not for you!

SECTION II
HOW TO MAKE KNIVES

The Loveless knife starts out as a 12-foot-long bar of hot-rolled and annealed 154CM tool steel about 1-1/4 inches wide and a rough .211 inch thick. Before bringing it to the shop, we have it cut into short lengths, usually 8 inches, 10 inches, or 14 inches long, depending on the knife. The short lengths are taken from the cut-off shop to a commercial grinding shop, where the stock is ground on either a **Mattison** or **Blanchard grinder.** These large machines are used to grind plane surfaces, and can be controlled quite closely by means of down-feed adjustments on the grinding head.

The stock is ground lightly on each side, removing about .010 inch per side, so that we end up with precision flat stock sized to .188/.190 inch, held parallel within .001 inch and with maximum bow of .010 inch.

(Years ago, I made knives directly from the hot-rolled bar, and often ran into trouble during heat treatment, when the work warped quite a bit. But gradually I learned that the surface of a hot-rolled bar is a sort of ''bark,'' which should be removed by grinding before further work, so taht you end up with sound steel.)

Grinding to a fixed, known dimension provides other advantages. It allows the use of pre-cut guards made up in advance on the milling machine, which is something I like to do when I just plain get tired of eating steel grit. Also, it gives a good surface for scribing, giving us a smooth bar to work with.

Scribe A Pattern

If you have any doubts, use a clamp.

We first place the pattern, a 4-inch Dropped Hunter, against the steel (1). Holding it down firmly (and if you have any doubts, use a clamp) to prevent slipping, we scribe all the way around the pattern with a carbide-pointed scribe, using heavy pressure to be sure to get a sharp line. After checking the layout, we take the blank to the **Burr-King belt grinder**, which has been set up in advance with an 8-inch contact wheel and a work support.

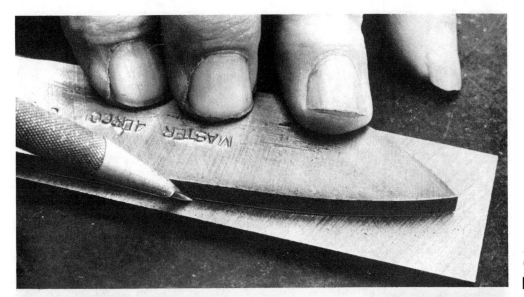

(1) Carefully scribe a pattern on the blank.

(2) Drift the belt to grind the tight curves.

Rough Grind

We've put a dull 60 grit belt on the grinder to use in this next step. The dull belt has already been used to grind bevels, and was pulled from that operation when it began building up too much heat in the work. The outline grinding is pure brute work. Resting the blade blank on the work support, and beginning at the butt-end of the blank, we take off the stock to within about 1/16 inch of the layout line, using heavy pressure against the belt. Because 154CM is not too heat-sensitive, allowing a bit of redness to build up at the grinding face won't hurt anything, especially since the first step in the later heat treatment will be a stress-relief at 1600 degrees F.

We progressively grind around the perimeter of the blade outline. Other workers often use a metal-cutting bandsaw, running at about 50 SFPM, but we've found that using a 2-HP, 3-phase belt grinder does the job more quickly and cheaply (because metal-cutting bandsaws don't come cheap). By feathering the edge of the belt out away from the edge of the contact wheel, we can cut the curved areas of the pattern (2), right down to within that same 1/16 inch of the line.

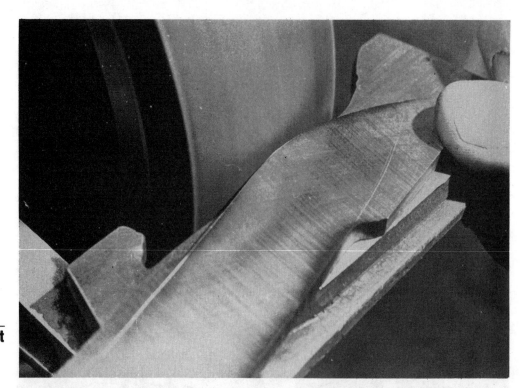

(3) Using a fresher 60 grit belt, grind until layout line disappears.

(4) Scribe a layout line on cutting edge of blade from point to choil.

Right now, when we get this close, we change belts, putting another used (but fresher) 60 grit belt on the Burr-King, and coming right on down to the line, finishing with a light touch of lessening pressure. And if you were watching this operation closely, you would see the layout line suddenly disappear, just as the belt gets to it. Right there is when to quit (3).

After doing the rough work with the 60 grit belts, we put a fresh 220 grit belt on the machine, and very lightly grind the edge of the blank again, ending up with a smooth surface that is ready for further layout.

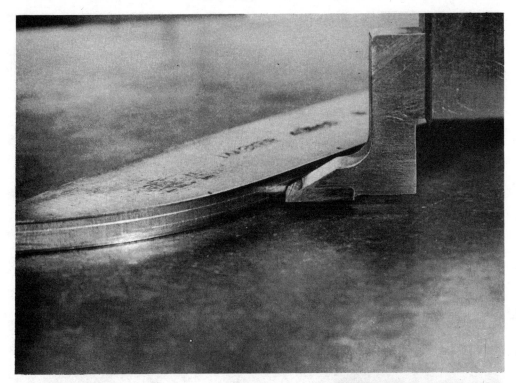

(5) **Turn knife over and repeat (4). The result will be two parallel lines on the cutting edge.**

(5A) **Vernier Caliper method. (Note: Line may not be as accurate as with the Mitutoyo Height Gauge).**

The ground blank is now placed on a precision granite surface plate, and, using a 6-inch **Mitutoyo Height Gauge,** we scribe lines on the face of the blank corresponding to the cutting edge (4). These lines are set in .065 inch from either surface, on the face of the blank, and scribed by laying the blank first on one surface and then reversing it to the outer surface. The result is a pair of lines .060 inch apart, which will control the bevel grinding in the next step of the work(5).

(Another way of scribing these lines is to use a **Vernier Caliper** (5A) which has had its points ground sharply. It is used just as a **Hermaphrodite Caliper** would be, to scribe a line a fixed distance in from a surface. Using this tool will give you a pair of lines a fixed distance apart, but not necessarily a pair of **straight** lines.)

At this point, before any further grinding, we clamp the permanent pattern back on the blade blank, precisely aligned, and take it to the drill press. We drill the fastener holes in the tang, using a #19 drill, which will cut a hole .166'' in diameter, a clearance hole for the 8-32NC screws to fasten the handle slabs in place. Next, using a #F drill, we drill the thong tube hole .257'' in diameter. Note that we do not drill the guard pin holes yet (6a).

The next step is grinding a small, forty-five degree bevel on the edge of the blank (6b), right down to the line adjacent to the wheel. Once again we see the line disappear just as we get to it, and we quit right there. The purpose of this bevel is twofold: it gives plenty of warning, when we get to grinding the master blade bevel, and it prevents the new, fresh 60 grit belt we'll use next from shearing its grains before it can get to work. If we were to begin grinding the master bevel with the new belt, without a lead-in bevel, the sharp edge of the blank would strip off much of the abrasive grain coated on the belt, before it could do any real work.

(6b) Grind a small 45 degree bevel on the blade edge.

(7) Grind the starting bevel on the tang.

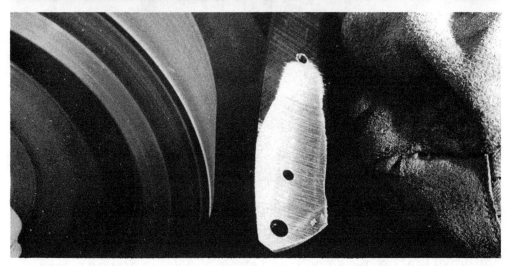

(8) Grind a smooth groove down both sides of the tang.

The next step is tapering the tang(7). We could go ahead and grind the blade bevel, but I would rather do that after tapering, because I get a better feel of the job if there isn't too much weight in the handle part of the blank.

(And if you've been laying off blade grinding for a few weeks, grinding the tang taper is a good way to get back into the swing of things.)

(9) Grind tang flat on the platen.

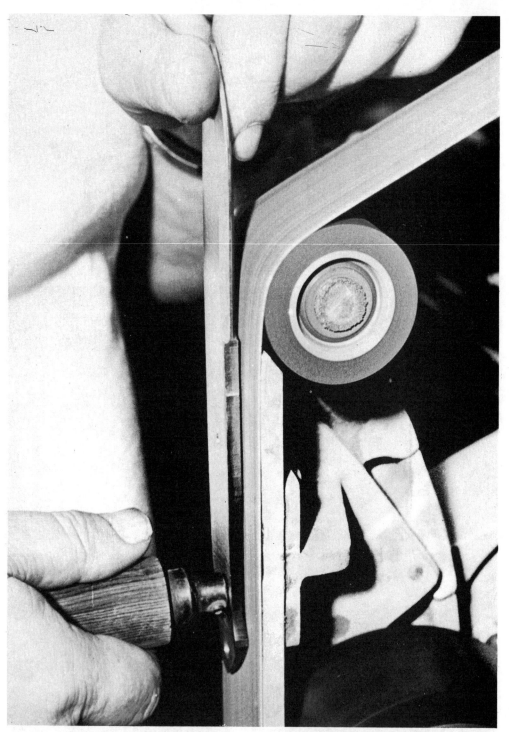

Note that in all grinding we are wearing safety glasses with tempered lenses. This needs saying very strongly. Grinding steel is hazardous, and the best eye protection is none too good.

With a 10-inch wheel in place, and a fresh 60 grit belt mounted, we begin grinding a groove along the tang (8). We take off more at the butt than up forward near the guard site, and we try to keep the bottom of that groove smooth and straight. We've ground a forty-five degree bevel back at the butt of the blade blank, and now we meet it with the groove, doing the same thing to both sides of the tang (9). The purpose of this step is to get as much stock as possible off the tang with the contact wheel rather than with the surface grinding on the platen, which is very severe on the belt (and on the operator). If we groove the tang well, only a very little work on the platen is needed to establish truly flat tang surfaces.

Now, finally, we are ready for the step that will make this chunk of steel begin to resemble a knife, the grinding of the master blade bevels. Using the 10-inch wheel with a fresh new 60 grit belt, we begin grinding free-hand (10a). It helps to keep your elbows braced closely against your ribs. I'm right-handed, so my right hand guides the work (10b) while my left hand supports it with just the thumb and first finger (10c). And as with the tang grinding, we set up the groove, from the point back to the area near the guard site. And because I'm right-handed, I pay special attention to the left-handed work; the objective is symmetry, and it is the mark of a well-ground blade.

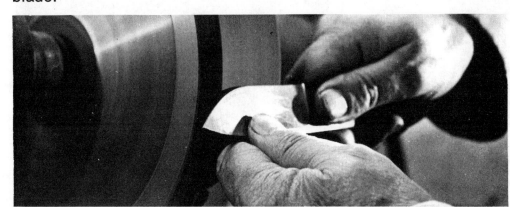

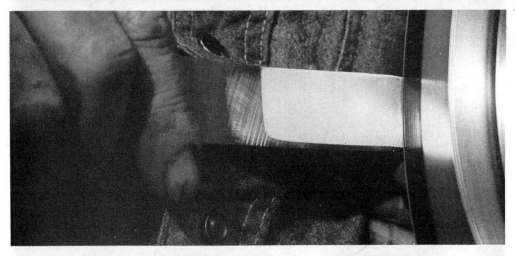

(10a) In grinding the blade, the objective is symmetry.

(10b) Note: Blade must have no deep scratches.

(10c) Note how just the thumb and first finger support the work.

When I have the bevels rough-ground, I change belts, and put on a fresh 220 grit belt, going over the bevels and smoothing them down. The object is to have no deep scratches in the bevels whatever, because such scratches would form stress risers, during the quenching, in heat-treat.

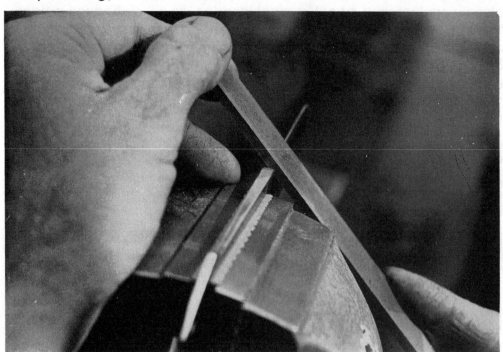

(11) Just behind the cutting edge, file a full radius to match the guard slot.

(12) Try-fit the guard.

All that remains before sending the blade out for heat-treat is locating and fitting the guard. We use brass, nickel silver and stainless steel, and the procedure is the same regardless of material. Just behind the end of the cutting edge, we carefully file a full radius to match the radius of the guard slot (11). Using a radius gauge as we work, we try-fit the guard (12) until it seats right into place. Then, using the Verniers, we scribe a centerline vertically up the guard (13), locate the punch points, and then center-punch the hole sites (14). Then we clamp up the trail assembly with a lever wrench, set it up in a drill press vise and carefully drill the holes for the guard pins, using a #42 drill (15). After

(13) Scribe a centerline up the guard.

(14) Center punch hole sites to guide drilling.

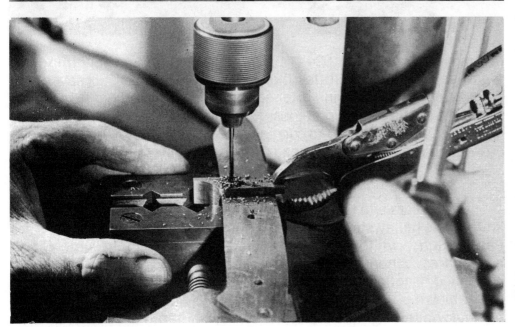

(15) Clamp guard and drill holes for pins.

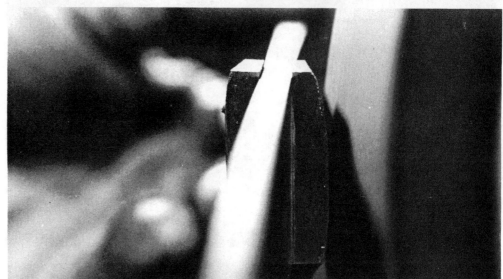

(16) Try-fit the guard pins.

(17) Rough shape the guard.

drilling, we fit try-pins .094'' (16) into the assembly to hold things together while we do a little bit of rough shaping (17). This saves a lot of heavy guard shaping after soldering, when the heat involved might break the solder joint loose. The guard is removed, the blade and guard are numbered to correspond with the customer's job order, and the blade is now ready to go out for heat-treating.

Heat Treatment

More years ago than I care to admit to, I heat-treated my first knife in the galley stove on board a small YO-class tanker, the ''Passiac Sun,'' while working for Sun Oil Company in the New York harbor area. When I got the blade about where I wanted it, I happened to notice that the fire in the stove was quite hot, oil-fueled under blown pressure. With a long-handled pair of tongs, I stuck the blade down through the top of the stove, right into the flame, and watched the work get a very pretty cherry red. Kept it in there maybe four or five minutes, brought it out, and plunged it into a 5-gallon bucket of refrigeration compressor oil, which was all the Chief Engineer had that I could use. I was some kind of lucky; the scale broke cleanly, settling to the bottom of the bucket and the blade came out a nice, even gray color all over. (I say lucky, because within a year I was having all kinds of trouble with heat-treatment, even though I had gone out and bought my own small bench furnace and done a little studying on the matter.) The bull-cook was breathing on me heavy, wanting to start the evening meal. He popped a batch of bread into the oven, and I popped my new hard blade right in there, too. Two hours later, the bread was done, and my knife blade was real pretty, sort of a pale straw violet, ready to be finished up.

I did finish up that first knife, used it aboard ship for quite a few months, and after coming ashore for good, went hunting with it many times. Would have had it yet, but it got up and walked out of the shop in Lawndale a few years ago. You know how those things happen, I'm sure.

Anyway, the point of this is that strangely enough, all these many years later, we still go through somewhat the same sort of process, except that I have the work done for me by a gent who knows what he's doing, using special vacuum equipment costing many, many thousands of dollars. Because, as the preacher said to the padre, "In our outfit, we gotta do things different."

My blades go to Sunnyvale, California, to the shop of **Pacific Heat Treat Company**, run by a fine gent named Billy Holt. This feller likes working with knife blades, and does the best job I know of. I just wish it hadn't taken me so long to find out about his work.

Anyway, our 154CM blades are placed in the vacuum furnace, hanging vertically on short wires. The furnace is closed and pumped down to a vacuum, and then the electric power turned on to bring the chamber up to temperature. After reaching 1,975 degrees F the blades are soaked for 30 minutes at temperature, the power shut down, and dry nitrogen flushed into the furnace, under positive pressure. This is the actual quench, and rapidly brings the blades down to room temperature, somewhere around 90 to 100 degrees F.

Now the furnace is opened, and the blades placed in a cold box, where they are brought down to -320 degrees F, very near absolute zero. This results in the maximum effect of quenching. But because 154CM actually works as a true high speed tool steel, we'll be getting more hardness during the draw, or temper, when the blades are hung back in the vacuum furnace, brought up to almost 1,000 degrees F, and held for two hours. Then they are brought down to room temperature, still in the furnace, and then once more taken up to the draw temperature of 1,000 degrees F for two more hours. This, of course, is the familiar 2 + 2 so much used by cutting tool heat treaters.

The result is a hardened blade, running about Rockwell C-61 to 63, depending on the particular melt of steel and variations in the alloying as it comes from the mill. I might add that **Crucible**, the folks who make 154CM, seem to do a pretty good job of keeping fairly constant alloy structure. We've been using this grade since the summer of 1972, and the response to heat treatment has been consistent and predictable.

(I should also add that although 154CM has earned a great record in the field, and although many custom knifemakers now use the grade, I don't think it is suitable for the fellow who decides, after reading this book, to make a knife or two for himself. It costs like the dickens and absolutely requires first-class heat treatment. On the other hand, the grade called **O-1 Oil Hardening** can be bought by the single piece at any machine shop supply house in the country. It is ground to close tolerances ready to use, and can be heat-treated, in a pinch, in the house furnace, if you can get the door open, or by your local friendly heat treater in the most simple equipment, for just a few dollars. The minimum charge for handling 154CM runs around $35, whether it's one blade or ten, by the way.)

Polish

When we get the knife back from heat-treating, the first step is to put a 220 grit belt on the grinder, with the vertical platen unit mounted in place. We carefully polish the flat sides of the blade(18), and also hit the sides of the tapered tang at the same time, to check for true flatness. If we've gotten any warpage during heat-treat, now's the time to take it out, by regrinding the tang with a fresh 60 grit belt.

(18) Carefully polish flat sides of the blade and check sides of the tang.

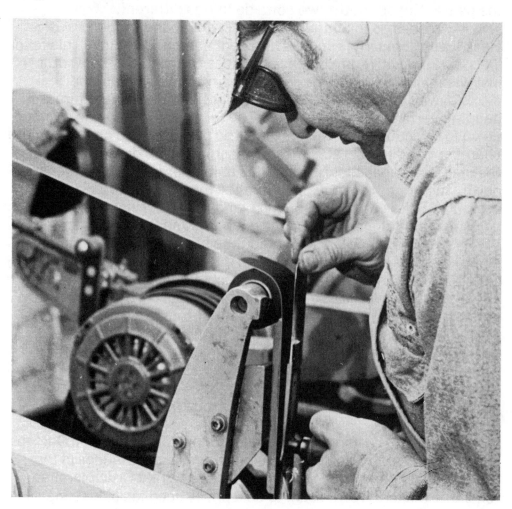

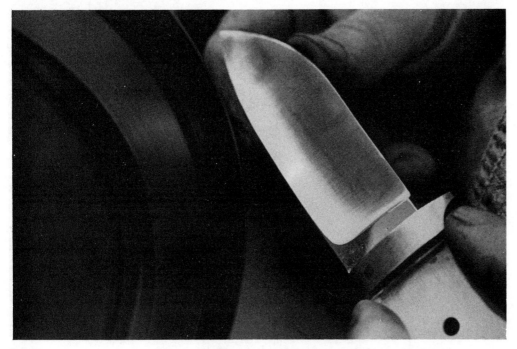

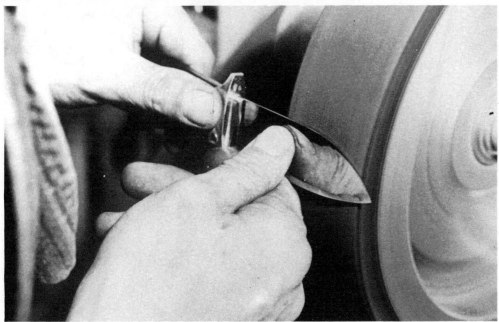

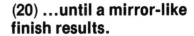

(19) Grind to finished size, eliminating scratches,

(20) ...until a mirror-like finish results.

After belt-polishing the flats, we check the blade for straightness, regrinding as needed, and then begin the polishing. Starting with a new 220 grit belt, we grind both sides of the blade completely, to finish size and thickness, being sure to remove any deep scratches which may have been left from the roughing work(19). Then we go to a 400 grit belt, going through the same process, eliminating the 220 grit scratches. Finally, using a very dull 500 grit extra-flexible belt, we begin working for a true polish, one you can see yourself in (it actually begins to act as a mirror, if you've done everything right(20)). Now is when those deep scratches, if there are any, will show up, and if you didn't catch them before, it's back to the 220 belt, and start the polishing work all over again. It's vital that the blade is cleaned up completely, but sometimes (yeah, even now, twenty some years after I started in this business) you just

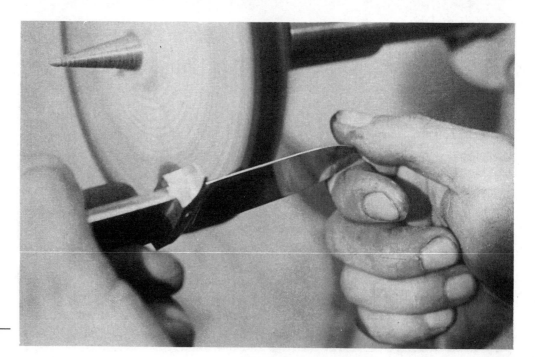

(21) Polish on the lathe.

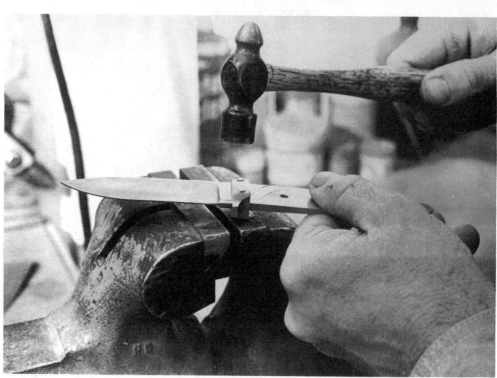

(22) Insert pins.

(23) Carefully peen over pins.

don't catch them all. The final result of the work with the dull 500 belt is a smooth, bright, and shiny blade, free of scratches, and now ready for polishing on the polishing lathe(21). The pictures show our Dropped Hunter with the guard attached, but this step is optional and can be done either just before or right after final polishing. However we do it, it isn't difficult; the pre-fitted guard is placed in position on the blade, clamped up, and then pinned(22). The pins are left slightly long and then the ends are carefully peened over(23). This peening closes up the guard on the blade, reducing the clearance gap to a minimum, and insures a mechanically strong joint.

We are now ready for soldering the guard in place. We've been using a grade of solder for several years now that seems to do the best job. Made by Eutectic Alloys, an outfit that has offices all over the country, it's **Eutectic's Grade 157**, a soldering alloy which contains no lead or tin (it's actually approved by most City Health Departments for use in stainless steel food processing equipment), so the resulting joint will stay bright and shiny in service. We use **Grade 157 Flux**, the stuff made by Eutectic to be used with this solder, and it's quite easy to work with.

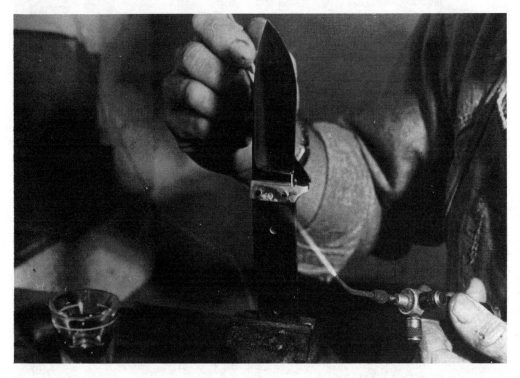

(24) Clamp blade vertically, joint up, guard protruding toward you.

(25) While heating the tang joint, wash it with muriatic acid.

Note from the picture (24) that the blade is clamped up in a bench vise vertically, point up, with the guard protruding toward you. Using a very compact oxy-acetylene torch, we direct the flame to the underside of the guard, where the guard and tang join, and quickly get the heat up to the melt temperature of the solder, 425 degrees F. As the heat starts to build, I wash the joint with a solder brush dipped in muriatic acid, and the hot acid helps clean the joint and burn out any residual wax from the polish job(25). After brushing with acid, we get a small amount of flux all along the joint, and as it begins to bubble, we get the solder rod into contact with the guard-ricasso joint. The solder begins flowing, and we move the solder rod along the joint on both sides, making sure we have enough solder melted into the joint to saturate the entire joint area(26). Now, quickly, do two things: take the torch away from the under-joint area, and brush the joint on both sides with the acid brush, brushing away all surplus solder and getting a clean neat minimum solder fillet where the blade meets the guard, all the way around.

(26) Make sure you have enough solder melted to saturate the entire joint area.

If there is any one thing that marks a good handmade knife, it is the appearnace of the solder joint around the guard. And to get a

(27) Insert knife into the Wilton vise.

(28) Clean the guard-blade joint in the regular vise.

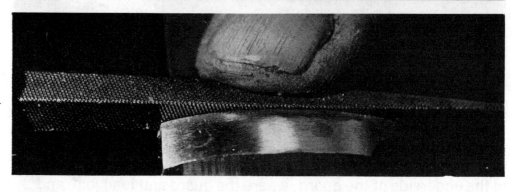

(29) Note where thumb pressure should be applied to insure true file action.

good neat joint that is strong, a close fit-up of the parts is vital. Careless work here will forever be obvious, and yet it is so easy to do a good job. And by the way, Allstate makes a solder very close to the 157 in application, called **Allstate 430**. Easier to get in some areas, too.

Now we take the knife to the workbench, to the vertical-mount **Wilton vise** (27). Using a square file with one face ground (the blind side, we call it), we remove the surplus solder from the tang side of the joint. Keep your file card handy and keep cleaning that file! Careful file work is vital here; it's easy to round off the rear surface of the guard, and that right away ruins the fit-up of the handle slabs to the guard face. When you've got the tang side of the joint cleaned up, get the knife into the regular vise (28) and clean up the guard-blade joint, the visible face of the guard. Note from the photo (29) that I keep my thumb pressure on the file here to insure straight, true file action.

Now, if you've been paying attention and doing things right, you ought to be ready for handle assembly. And so we are. Since we make what are known as "full-tang" knives in this shop, what follows applies only to that kind of knife.

Now, if we have a tapered tang, and the guard is assembled perpendicular to the blade centerline, it must follow that the angle formed by the rear face of the guard and the tang surface is slightly more than 90 degrees, right? Yep, exactly, and you have to allow for it in setting up your handle parts. First comes a piece of .030" thick red vulcanized fiber (and the reason is that I like a bit of color on my knives, like just a touch of lipstick on a pretty girl). Lay the fiber down on a flat surface, with a straight edge up against the guard, and, using a yellow pencil, draw the outline of the tang on the fiber. Then take another piece of fiber, turn the knife over, and do it again on that piece. Now cut the fiber to the rough shape of the knife handle (and for this I use a pair of straight-cut aviation sheet metal snips). Now set the fiber to one side, take your handle slabs and fit each of them to the same guard-face/tang-surface angle(30). You'll note (31) that I use a set-up on the **Clausing Vertical Mill** to do this

(30) Fit each handle slab to the same guard-blade/tang-surface angle.

(31) Set-up on Clausing Vertical Mill.

job (32), but you can do it almost as easily with a flat bastard file (33) or on the platen of the grinder. The important thing is to get a snug, tight fit, with no visible gaps (34). Now, when both the fiber piece and the handle slab are fitted to the guard face, the resulting trial assembly is clamped up and taken to the drill press, in a fixture we built here to keep the blade centerline perpendicular to the drill (35). Note that we block up the job from underneath to keep the drilling pressure from forcing the hole away from vertical. We carefully drill the fastening holes with the #19 drill, using the hardened tang as a drill jig and then, on an adjacent drill press, we drill the #F hole at the rear of the tang, for the thong tube. Right here, we take the fixture back to the bench, press fit pins into both of the fastener holes and then take the clamp off. Then it's to the high-speed bandsaw, where we cut away (36) the handle and fiber material to within about 1/8'' of the tang (37). Now you have one side of the handle assembly ready for epoxy, almost. Next, do the other side the same way, clamping in the fixture, drilling through the tang, pinning and sawing to the outline of the tang.

At this point, both sides of the knife handle are almost ready for the epoxy and assembly. All that remains is countersinking the fastener holes on the outer faces of the handle slabs to the proper depth (38).

(33) Fitting up with a flat bastard file.

(34) Make sure the set-up is snug and tight.

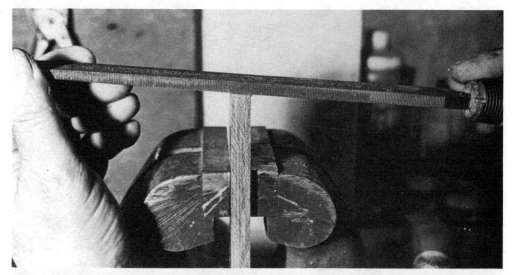

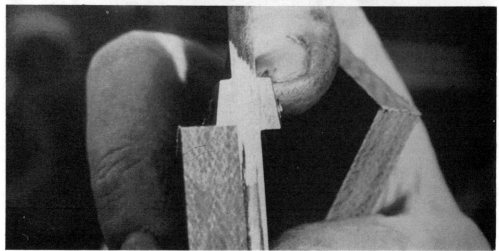

(35) Fixture built to keep the blade centerline perpendicular to the drill.

(36) Use the high-speed bandsaw to cut away the handle and fiber material.

(37) Cut to within 1/8'' of the tang.

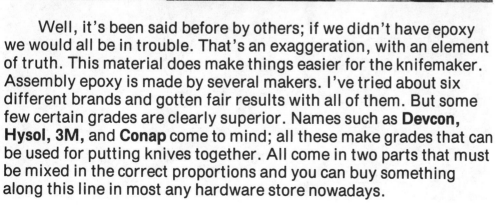

Well, it's been said before by others; if we didn't have epoxy we would all be in trouble. That's an exaggeration, with an element of truth. This material does make things easier for the knifemaker. Assembly epoxy is made by several makers. I've tried about six different brands and gotten fair results with all of them. But some few certain grades are clearly superior. Names such as **Devcon, Hysol, 3M,** and **Conap** come to mind; all these make grades that can be used for putting knives together. All come in two parts that must be mixed in the correct proportions and you can buy something along this line in most any hardware store nowadays.

(38) Countersink the fastener holes on the outer faces of the handle slabs.

It happens that we are using both **Conap's Easypoxy** and **3M's Grade 2216A** here in this shop now. Regardless, once the stuff is mixed, you carefully coat the inner side of the near slab with a shortened solder brush (and be sure to grab a clean one, not the brush you used for soldering). Get a thin coat onto every bit of the slab surface, put your fasteners up through the slab, and drop the nearside fiber liner down on the screws, seating it against the epoxy coating on the Micarta slab. Now coat the inner side of the red fiber, and then place the tang of the knife down on the screws, carefully, being sure that everything lines up properly(39). Close it up, and then coat the off-side of the tang. Now put the thong tube in position, and seat it home (so the far end is at least even with the near-side slab) (40) and then put the off-side red fiber liner down on the screws, and right against the tang surface. Then coat the fiber with epoxy(41), set the off-side slab in place, and close it up snug. Next, place the nuts on the screw ends, run them down snug, and tighten up as tight as you can get them with a screwdriver, holding the assembled knife in the vise(42).

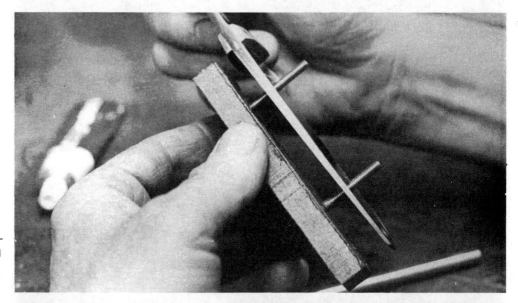

(39) Align carefully when placing the tang down on the screws.

(40) Position the thong tube and seat it home.

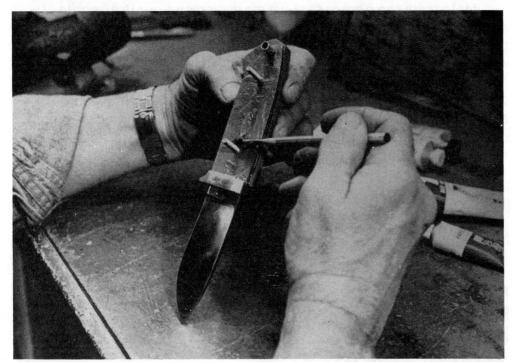

Most of the commonly used epoxies need several hours to set up to maximum strength, so set the knife aside overnight, and go in and pay some attention to your wife, who is probably getting a little tight around the eyes about now.

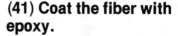

(41) Coat the fiber with epoxy.

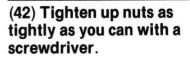

(42) Tighten up nuts as tightly as you can with a screwdriver.

When the epoxy is hard, we take the set-up assembly to the belt grinder, where we have mounted a fresh sharp 40 grit belt. Running against the contact wheel, we grind down the surplus handle material close to the tang edge, leaving very little but being careful not to touch steel with that 40 grit belt. These coarse belts cut deep scratchy grooves, and it's hard work to clean them up again. Better not to let such belts touch your semi-finished tang surfaces at all. Oh, by the way, a new 40 grit belt does a fine job of making hamburger out of finger tips and other odd assorted parts of the hands, so (once more), BE CAREFUL. Grinding cuts are particularly painful and take several days to heal.

(43) Start blocking out the handle shape on the contact wheel.

Note from the photos that we start blocking out the handle shape on the contact wheel (43), again using the abrasive belt to do the hard work. Since we shape the **LOVELESS** knife handle a certain way, we've learned how to start the curved surfaces with sequential movements on the wheel (44), actually doing perhaps 90 percent of the shaping on the belt grinder (45). Bear in mind that you can always take material off, but once off, you can't put it back. So be careful, work gently, removing small amounts of (in this case) Micarta, and checking often for the shape you want.

(44) Start the curved surfaces with sequential movements on the wheel.

(45) Almost all of the shaping is done on the belt grinder.

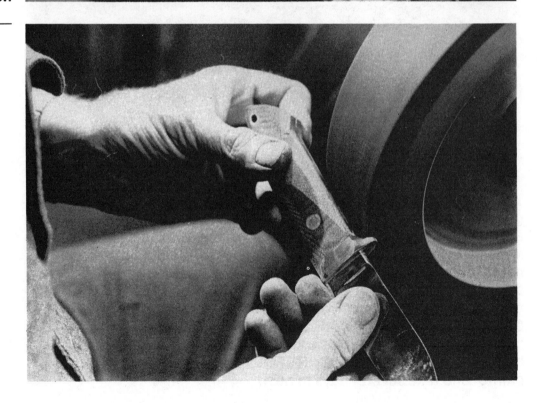

When ycu've done all the work you can on the belt, it's time to go back to the work bench. I smooth up the rough-ground knife handle on a free, slack belt, using a narrower-than-usual 220 grit extra-flexible belt (46). Note that the belt conforms to the curved surfaces, and just smooths up the job (47).

If I've done everything right, only a little bit of work is left to do now. Clamp the knife up in the vise, and carefully clean up the guard curve (48). Next, using a type of file called the **Crossing file**, I clean up the recurve area of the lower butt (where, in use, your little finger

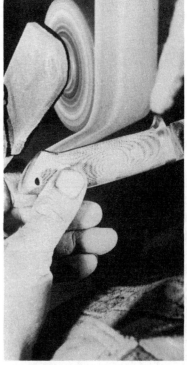

(46) **Smooth the rough-ground knife on a free, slack belt.**

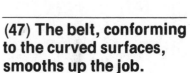

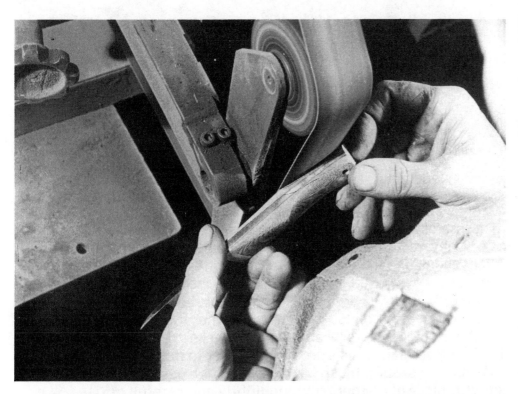

(47) **The belt, conforming to the curved surfaces, smooths up the job.**

(48) **Carefully clean up the guard curve.**

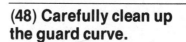

(49) Use a Crossing file to clean up the recurve area of the lower butt.

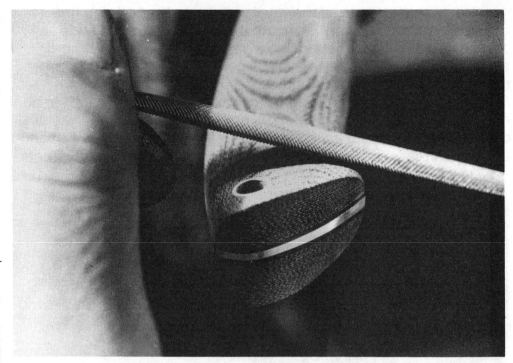

(50) Use a shoeshine motion to sand the entire handle.

must have leverage) (49). After doing all the file work on the handle, we use narrow strips of emery cloth (sold as bench rolls by all the major producers of abrasives). We sand the entire handle, using a kind of shoeshine motion (50). Start out with 320 grit, and then finish all over with 500 grit, being sure to check the surface of the handle very carefully against a strong light, because the reflection will show up the smallest scratches. Another thing to watch for is how the escutcheon surfaces clean up. These are metal (brass and steel), and scratches here are much harder to deal with. To avoid undercutting around these fastener ends, we use the abrasive with a flat, stiff piece of leather, rubbing lightly and carefully (51).

(51) Use a flat, stiff piece of leather, rubbing lightly and carefully, on the escutcheon surfaces.

Now the knife is ready for the trademark. I've never liked the idea of stamping highly-stressed tool steel, and have been using the **KMER** process to trademark my knives since about 1966. Prior to that I used a **Burgess Vibratool**, and etched my name and shop location onto the blade by hand. But the photosensitive system made by Kodak (**KMER: Kodak Metal Etch Resist**) captured my heart and mind strongly, and I've never seen anything since that I like as well. Actually, the KMER materials simply replace older materials to form what the etcher calls the ''ground.'' The mark is still made the age-old way, by the action of acid, eating away at the steel to a controlled depth.

The first step in getting the blade ready for etching is cleaning. I use **MEK (methyl ethyl ketone),** and the little squares of processed cotton your wife uses for removing her makeup. They're called **COETS** Quilted Cosmetic Squares, and cost about a buck-fifty for 150 pieces. I saturate the cotton with MEK, and rub the near-side surface of the blade until it literally squeaks(52). Inevitably, there is an invisible coat of wax or skin oils on the blade, that must be removed before anything else can be done. Rub hard, and when you hear it squeak, it's clean. The MEK evaporates very quickly, leaving a shiny surface. Now I coat the area to be etched with a thinned coat of KMER, an amber, syrupy-looking fluid. I roll the blade back and forth some while holding it horizontally, being sure to obtain a smooth, level coating, evening it out with the tip of the medicine dropper I used to apply it(53). All this takes only about ten seconds, and then I hang the knife vertically, with a nail through the thong hole (and that's one of the big reasons why most every LOVELESS knife has a thong tube; it makes things easy, handling the blades and knives here in the shop). This allows the surplus KMER to drain away from the etching area, leaving the smooth even coat we must have. The knife is allowed to hang for about 15 minutes, while the coating is air-drying, and then it's placed in a bench oven running at 180 degrees F, where it stays for 10 minutes. This heat, or baking, dries the coating and makes it less easily damaged in subsequent handling.

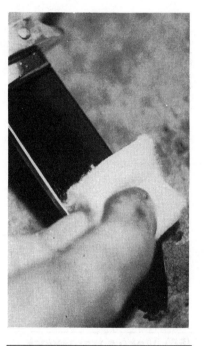

(52) **Rub the near-side surface of the blade until it squeaks.**

(53) **Even out the KMER with the tip of the medicine dropper used to apply it.**

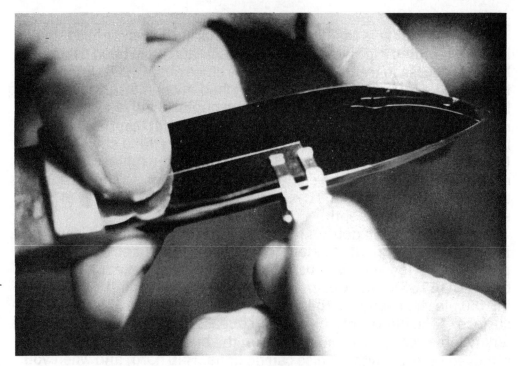

(54) Clamp the photo-positive of the trademark on the blade with styling clips.

After cooling down to room temperature, I place the photo-positive of my trademark, in actual size, on the blade in the proper place, and clamp it there with modified hair clips, known as styling clips to your wife, who uses them in fussing with her hair (54). Now I place the blade in a little jig, or framework, made out of a small can and a plastic tray, on which I mount an ultraviolet light projector (55), the kind used by rockhounds to look at those funny rocks that glow in the dark. And right here is the secret, if there is one, of the whole KMER process: the coating is sensitive to the UV light, which polymerizes the material when exposed to long-wave UV radiation.

(55) Make a framework on which to mount an ultraviolet light.

(56) Use a small camel's hair brush to coat the blade with clear lacquer.

After UV exposure, the blade is placed in a beaker of KMER Developer and developed. If you can consider the blade to be an exposed film, needing development, you will understand the principle involved. We develop for 60 seconds, and then, after rinsing off the surplus developer, place the blade back in the oven for a post-bake. Note that the developed image appears during the rinse, and that the coating is very soft and easily damaged at this point. The post-bake takes ten minutes, and then we take the blade out of the oven and let it cool down to room temperature. Next I take a small camel's hair brush, and (very carefully!) coat the entire blade with clear lacquer, to within about 1/8th of an inch of the image(56).

(57) Drop acid into the image with a medicine dropper.

The purpose of this lacquer coating is important: when I drop the etching acid on the image, and it begins working, it bubbles up and spatters tiny drops of acid all over the adjacent areas on the blade. If it weren't protected with lacquer, the blade would show little dark spots, sort of like measles, all over your pretty shiny knife. So we mask off, and then block up the knife on the bench so it's horizontal and then drop acid into the image with a medicine dropper(57). Cover the image completely, but don't use too much acid(58). Let the acid work for about a minute, and then suck most of it back up into the medicine dropper, and rinse the rest off, quickly, under running water.

Now check the job (59) for a good etch. It wants to be dark, and sharp all over(60). If we've done everything right, the result is the nicest trademark I know of, and more importantly, a mark which does not weaken the blade at all, as a stamped name would.

(58) The image should be covered completely without using too much acid.

(59) **Check the job for a good etch.**

(Yeah, I know — there are lots of knives around with stamped trademarks. But do this sometime: ask a metallurgist about notch-sensitive tool steels, and stress risers, and stuff like that and you'll learn why I don't stamp my blades, ever.)

Okay, now we have a finished knife. Well, almost. All that remains is to give it a light buffing on the polishing lathe, on a loose cotton wheel charged with green chrome rouge, working up that delightful crisp shine so adored by us knife freaks.

Now, pass go, and move directly to the sheath section of this book, and get your little beauty ready to go hunting, or whatever.

(And by the way, temperatures in this section of the book are in degrees Fahrenheit. The metric system hasn't caught on here yet, and I'm gonna drag my feet, screaming, into the new world order, if forced, but not happily. The problem is, I'm used to doing things the old way.)

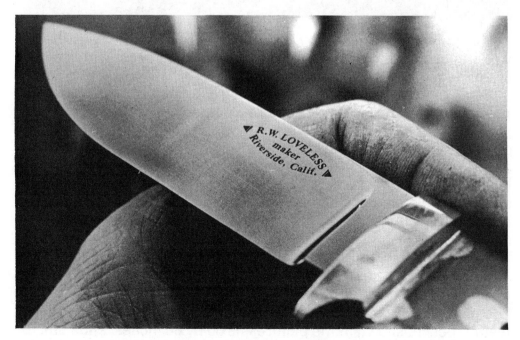

(60) **The etch should be dark and sharp all over.**

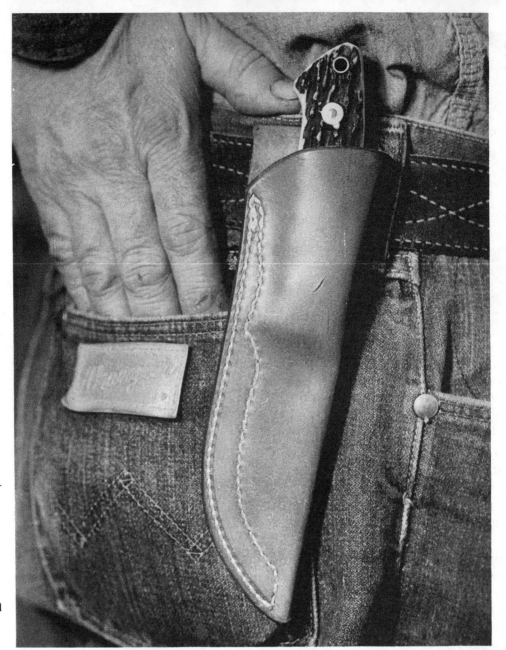

A pouch sheath for your knife, made in twenty-three simple steps. A sheath of this type will protect better than many others. A leather thong (if there's a place for one) would be a nice touch.

Just as you can make any kind of soup provided you have the water to begin with, to make a sheath you have to begin with leather of a certain type, grade, and size.

You'll need cowhide, in a grade called shoulder, or back, of about nine ounce thickness. **Tandy Leather Company**, with stores just about everywhere, should be able to furnish this grade of cowhide, along with the few tools you'll need. Plan on obtaining a small, pointed, very sharp knife, a grooving tool to make the fold lines, and an edger to smooth up the edges once you have the sheath completed and stitched. Also obtain a can of **Barge Cement**. Your local shoemaker can sell you a can, if Tandy is temporarily out of stock.

How much leather should you buy? I would suggest a piece at least 8 inches wide by 16 inches long; any less and you might be crowded. Next, clear off a space on your workbench or on the kitchen table, so you'll have enough room to really work. My own leather bench, shown in the pictures, is 30 by 80 inches, and I still feel a bit cramped now and then.

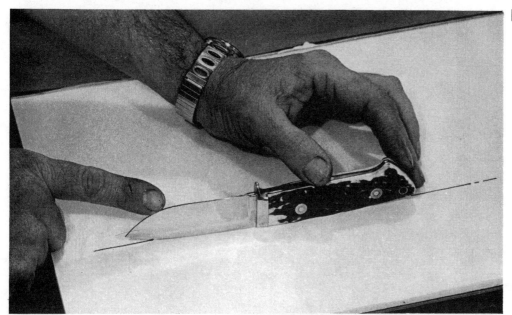

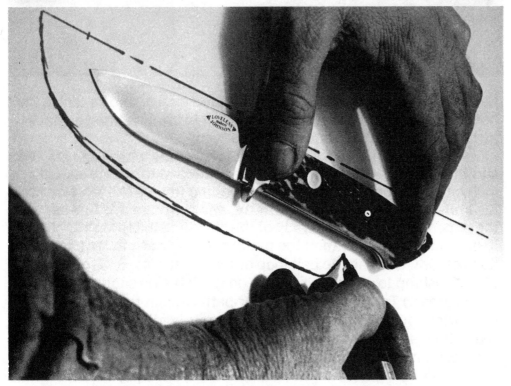

(1) Lay knife on scribed base line.

(2) Roll knife carefully to right, make dashed series of guide lines about 1-inch away.

Your first job will be to make up a paper pattern for the body of the sheath. It isn't tricky, and it sure beats making a mistake that will send you out for more leather. Get a sheet of stiff paper the same size as your piece of leather. Then, just to the right of the vertical center of the paper, draw a dashed line using a straight edge for a guide. This will be your centerline, the basic controlling line of your pattern. Next, set the knife on this line(1), point toward you and cutting edge up, and very carefully, without allowing the knife to slip, roll it to your right. The cutting edge should now face to the right, away from the centerline. Holding the knife in place with your left hand, and beginning about an inch below the point, draw a line up and around your knife(2). Keep this line about an inch away from

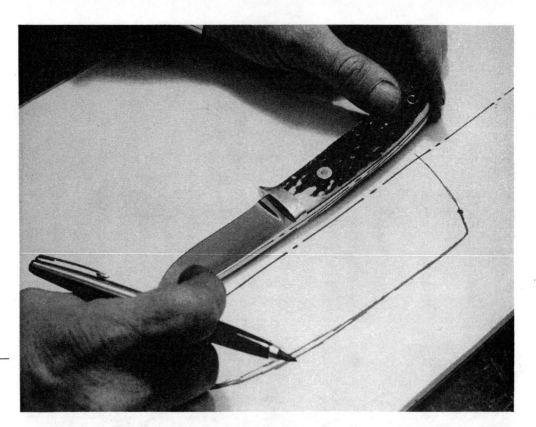

(3) Roll knife to left and repeat the above procedure.

the knife's outline, past the edge, then the guard, and as far up the handle as you think you want your sheath to be. The line you have just drawn will be the edge of your pattern.

Again place the knife back on the centerline where you started, and this time roll it to your left(3). Beginning at the same spot, an inch below the point, draw a corresponding line up the left side of the knife, always about an inch away, and continue this line as far up the paper as you want the body of the sheath to extend. Put the knife to one side now and extend the pattern line upward to form the back flap that will become the belt loop of the sheath (4). (Editor's note: Those wishing to wear their knives on the left side should reverse this process.) To complete the paper pattern, join the lines up, cut the pattern out with shears, and then carefuly fold along the centerline, at the same time folding down the tongue to check the fit and positioning of the back flap.

Before going any further, put the knife in the paper pattern and make sure you have something that looks like a sheath, if only vaguely(5). The secret, if there is any, to making a good pouch sheath is carefully checking the pattern to the knife. Once you are sure you have what you want, lay the paper down on your piece of leather, on the rough side, and transfer the shape of the pattern onto the leather with a ball-point pen(6).

Check and Double Check

At this point, you still have a chance to make any corrections needed on the pattern, so now is the time for one last check to make sure the pattern covers the knife and the belt loop is high (or low) enough and big enough to fit your belt. Check the pictures, and note the way the knife is placed in the folding pattern.

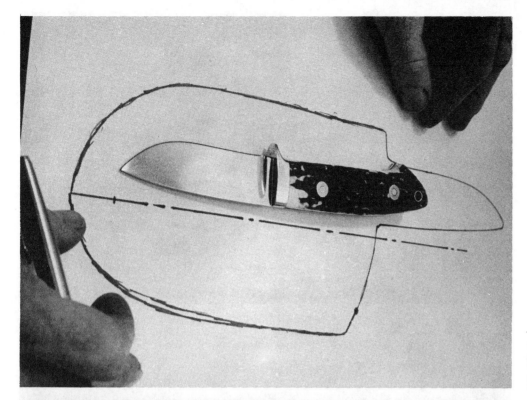

(4) Be certain to include the belt loop area in your pattern.

(5) Check knife against pattern to see if it will fit. Now is the time to correct mistakes.

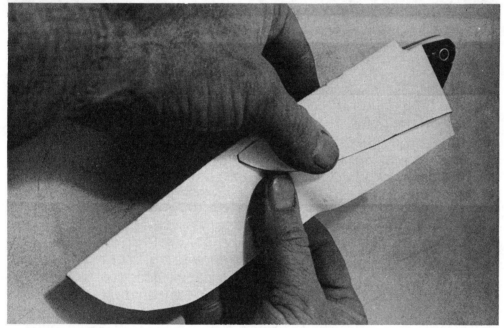

I've made maybe a few hundred different paper patterns since the early days in Delaware, and still I manage to mess things up on occasion. These days, I have heavy stiff patterns made up to fit the various Loveless models (note that we're using the 4-inch Dropped Hunter as a model in these pictures), but every now and then I have to make up something special for a customer, and this method of making up a paper pattern is the only way I know that works. So my advice is do it right, fit it up well, use the best grade of cowhide you can get your hands on, glue it up and stitch it carefully, and you'll get yourself a piece of outdoor gear that will last you your whole lifetime, with just a little care.

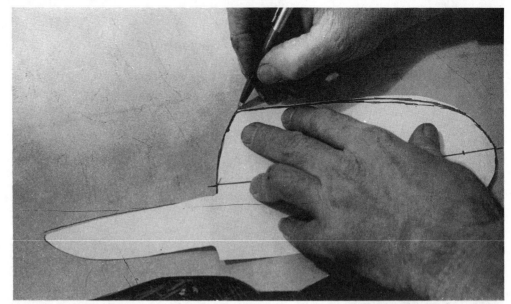

(6) Transfer pattern to leather with pen.

(7) Cut leather carefully. Try to make cuts flush.

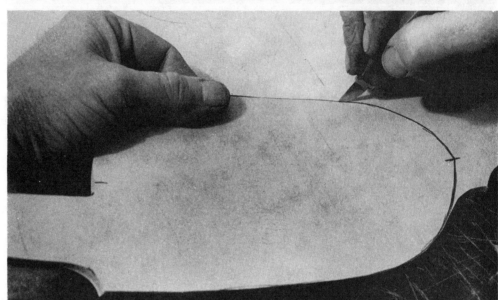

Ready To Cut

Okay, the pattern suits you, you've got it laid down on the rough side of the leather, and you're ready to start cutting(7). Now the knife work begins, and you'd better have a good tool to use. Mine is the **Stanley Slimknife**, #28-109, and my blade shape is the pointed #28-133 style. Here's a tip: when you've got the knife as sharp as you can get it on your hone, put it on the buffer and polish the cutting edge bevels, using a muslin wheel charged with green chrome rouge. Now it will cut through tough leather without drag, and you'll have no trouble following your lay-out lines. By the way, if you are working on your wife's kitchen table, you sure as hell better have some kind of plywood or something to cut into. Take my word for it, there ain't no knife sheath worth that kind of trouble. Also, since I have to figure I'm writing this article for everyone from fresh pilgrims to old mossybacks, I'll throw this in: make some practice cuts on a scrap piece of leather, before working on your sheath blank, especially if you have never tried this kind of business before.

(8) Scribe centerline on leather blank, just as you did for pattern.

(9) Cut folding grooves on either side of base line.

Start Slicing

Moving right along, once you have the sheath blank cut out, lay down a centerline that matches the centerline you made on the pattern(8). Lay the knife on the leather, where you want it vertically, and make a little mark with a ball-point pen right where the guard is. Now, with your grooving tool, cut folding grooves beside the centerline from the guard point right down the blank to the bottom (9). Space these grooves about 1/8 inch to either side of the centerline, as shown in the pictures. These grooves will allow the leather to fold ninety degrees twice and thus form the lower blade pocket of the sheath. Next, figure where you want the back flap to fold to form the belt loop, and cut a single groove along that line, again so the leather can fold easily without strain or cracking(10). Fold the flap over and mark off the area to be glued, leaving room for the belt loop itself. Before gluing up the belt loop, cut two more grooves along the centerline a bit further away from it than 1/8 inch, almost to the top of the sheath. These two upper grooves allow the upper part of the sheath to take the round form of the knife handle (11).

55

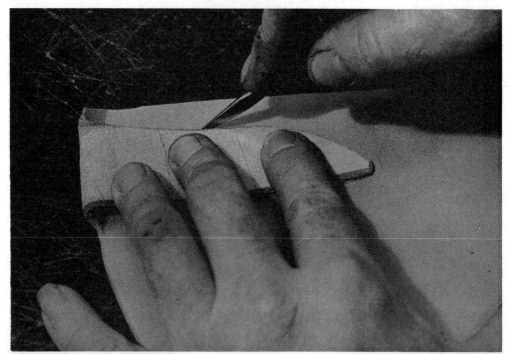

(10) Scribe off belt loop area on back of sheath.

(11) Cut grooves for handle fit — allow more room than you did for fold.

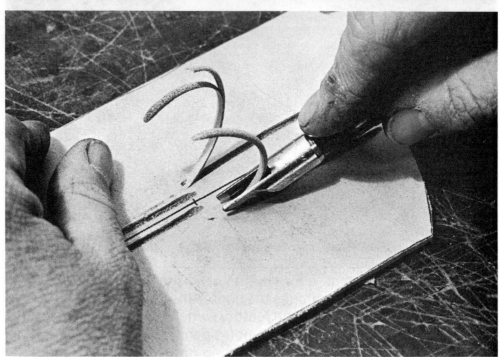

Groove And Glue

Lay the **Barge Cement** down on the belt loop flap (12) and on the body of the sheath, and stay inside the marked-off area if you care at all how nice your sheath will look.

At this point, you should have the two sets of grooves cut on the rough, inside surface and a single groove cut at the top of the belt loop on the smooth side of the leather. Refer to the pictures frequently, from start to finish, so you won't groove or glue up the wrong side of the leather. Don't make your grooves too deep, just deep enough to do the job right. Use only enough glue to thoroughly wet the surface of the leather, and no more. The Barge can has a brush on the cap, and you can use it to make a smooth, even coating

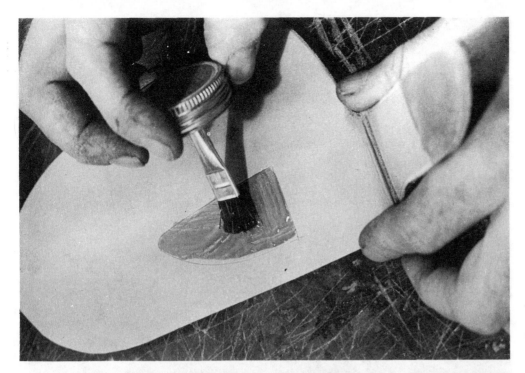

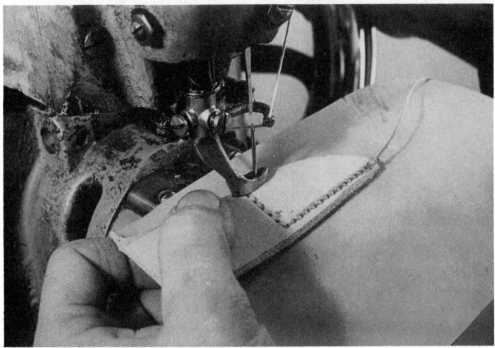

(12) Use the Barge Cement to glue down belt loop.

(13) It's stitching time. Local shoemaker can help.

of glue. Allow the glue to dry for several minutes, until it's almost dry to the touch, and then fold the belt loop flat and close it down. Here in my shop, I tap it down with a rubber mallet, but you can use any kind of hammer you happen to have handy, provided you protect the sheath surface with a scrap piece of leather. You'll notice now that I stitch down the flap with a heavy duty stitching machine(13), but this job can also be done by hand with one of the hand awls like the **C.A. Myers Lock Stitch Sewing Awl** sold by the Tandy folks. In a pinch, the flap can be locked down with **DOT Speedy Rivets**, although a stitched job looks much nicer to me. Here's a hint: after gluing down the flap, take it to your local friendly shoemaker and ask him to stitch it down for you.

57

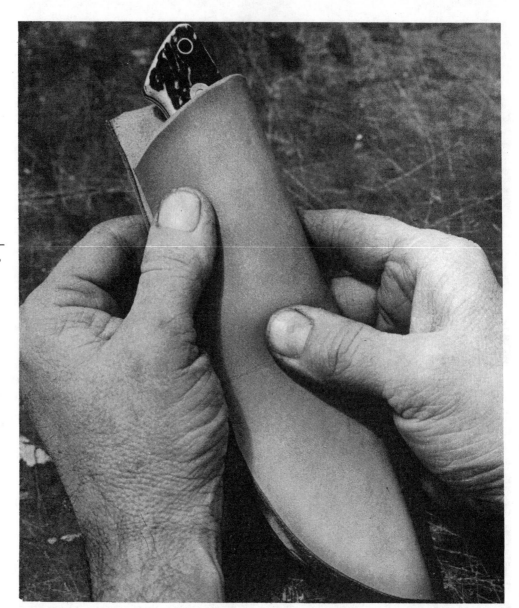

(14) Wet forming begins. Mold carefully with fingers.

Wet Forming

Now we come to a vital step in the making of a pouch sheath: the first wet forming. Good cowhide possesses a unique property. It stretches when slightly wet, and holds whatever shape you mold it to. So now you turn on the hot water tap (hot water works best, although I don't know why), and put the sheath under it, getting it just wet enough to turn dark in color, but not soaking wet. Fold the sheath side together to form the pocket, and get the knife into it, about in the position you want it to be. Mold the damp leather in against the knife, especially around the guard and around the handle(14). Press the leather against the blade, on each side, enough to get an imprint of the edge on the surface of the cowhide. Be sure to have your hands clean while you're molding the leather, because any dirt or stains you get on the leather during this operation won't come out, period.

When you are satisfied that you've molded the leather down on the knife to suit you, take the knife out of the wet-formed pouch, and wipe it off dry. Even if your knife is made out of 440C or 154CM, nothing will stain it like hot, wet leather.

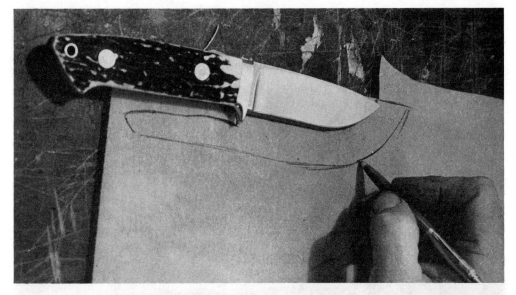

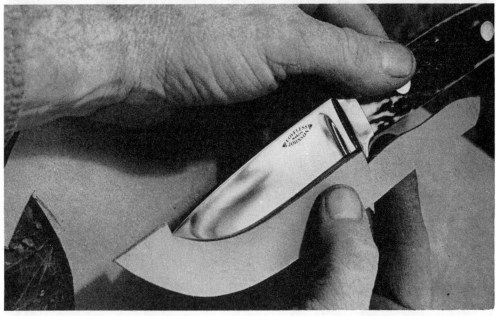

(15) Using knife as guide, sketch out welt piece.

(16) Check welt against blade. Allow cam for good fit.

Making The Welt

While the sheath is drying, you're going to make the welt. That's the piece of thick, stiff leather that lies between the two sides of the sheath, along the cutting edge, which provides the major structural strength of the pouch style sheath. I've used a grade of sole leather called **Tioga Oak Prime Grainflex**, bought from MacPherson's here in the Los Angeles area, and it's the best for this job. If you have trouble getting sole leather, ask the shoemaker to sell you a halfsole blank, such as he uses to resole work shoes. Note from the pictures that you lay the knife against the material, and draw a line with a ball-point pen to match the outline of the knife itself, and then another line about an inch away, from the point to the top of the sheath at the handle area(15). Now this is thick, stiff leather, but cut it out carefully, and check the inner line for fit against the knife(16). Very important: note that on the inner line, just above the guard, we draw in a little curve. This part of the welt becomes a sort of cam, that serves, in use, to help keep the knife from falling out of the sheath.

59

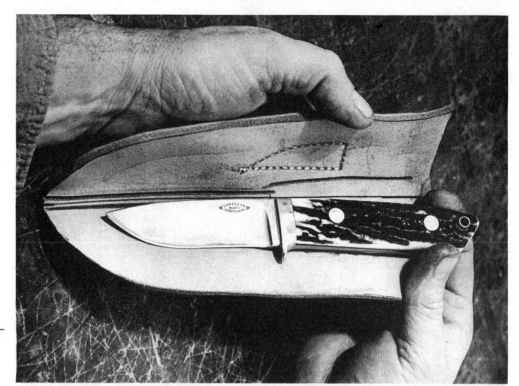

(17) Will the welt fit with the blade in place?

(18) Welt fit, cam, and position are all crucial. Trace welt piece on sheath side.

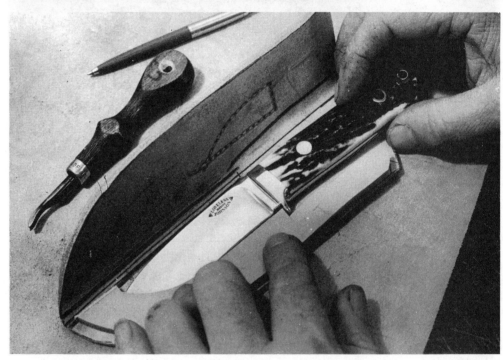

When the welt suits you, put the knife back into the now almost dry sheath, being careful to set it into the formed pouch (17). Now set your welt in against it, hold it in place, take out the knife (carefully, so that nothing changes position), open up the folded sheath, and mark off the position of the welt (18). Now coat the side of the welt that sets against the outer face of the sheath with the Barge Cement (19) and glue up the matching area on the inside of the outer face. After the glue dries, join the two parts together, and tap the joint with your hammer. You'll note that at this point I stitch the welt to the outer face on a stitcher, and I suggest you do the same (20).

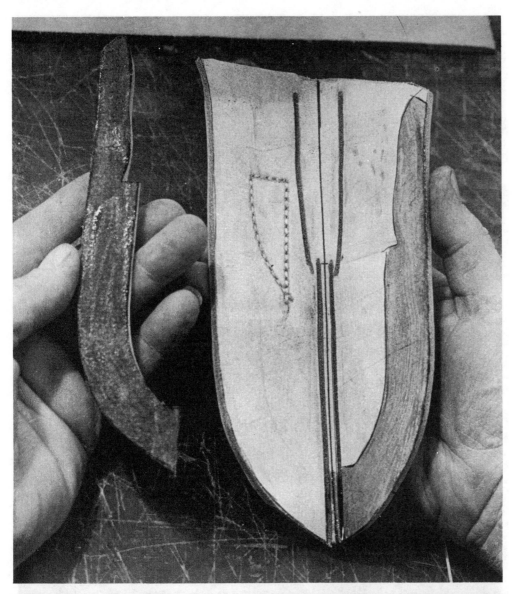

(19) Glue welt in place. Barge Cement is best.

(20) Stitch down welt. Use machine if possible, but hand awl works fine.

61

(21) Glue up top of welt. Use fairly thick coat.

(22) Stitch down sheath side through welt. Pattern stitching might add nice touch.

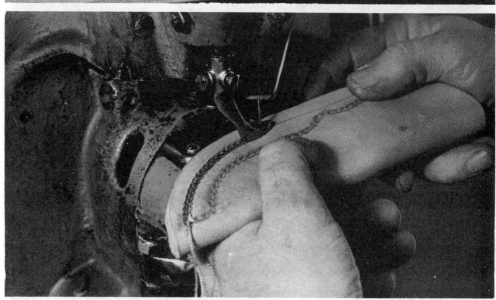

Still More Stitching

You are now about to learn that leather work can be a bit tedious at times. No matter, dues must be paid, and this stitching of the welt is important on the finished job.

With the welt stitched in place, put the knife back in the sheath, close it up (bring both sides together, in other words), and check the formed pouch for fit. Move the knife out of the pouch, and see if it feels like it wants to move freely, once past the camming curve on the welt. If everything feels good, you are ready to glue up the welt to the inside of the sheath. Again, let the Barge get almost dry to the touch, join the two surfaces together, and hammer them up tight (21).

I'm tempted to tell you to just stitch up the sheath, but before I do, I guess I'd better point out that by this time you should have along the rear edge of the sheath a structure of leather almost a half-inch thick, made up of the two faces of the sheath plus the welt. If you're careful, you can now go ahead and finish up the stitching by hand, with your hand awl, making certain to pull up each stitch to form a good, tight lock.

Or you can do what I did until just a few years ago, before I was able to get my own **American Straight Needle Stitcher**: go back to that friendly shoemaker, and ask him to run a line of stitching right up the back of the sheath (22). He'll know exactly what's needed; and it will take him all of a minute or two to do this job for you.

You can see from the pictures what you should have by now. The sheath is almost complete, and most of the job is done. Now once again wet the sheath in hot water, just slightly, and start working your knife in and out several times. Do some more molding with your fingers as the leather is drying, and, finally, trim off any excess leather, leaving about 1/4-inch beyond the stitch line for looks and strength (23). It's also a good idea to force the belt you will be wearing through the belt loop, making sure it's a good fit, so your knife won't be flopping all over as you pile out of the jeep to nail that big buck.

Finishing Touches

After the sheath is thoroughly dried out, I put it in a small bench oven here in the shop, running at about 180 degrees F, and heat it up. Then I dip it in a fifty-fifty mixture of **Neatsfoot Oil** and **Sellari's Cold Wax**. Let the hot, dry leather soak up a little of this mixture for just a few seconds, then quickly dry off the surplus with a rag inside and out. Work the knife in the sheath a few times, to be sure everything fits, and buff a coat of **Holt's Finishing Wax** onto the sheath.

Finally, when all is done, go to the hone and start sharpening the knife itself, which is the last thing I do here in my own shop, and the reason I have all my fingers and toes.

**MAKING A KNIFE AT
THE MORAN FORGE**

**(1) The Moran forge is
ideal for bladesmithing.**

The Moran forge is of stone, fire brick, and fire clay. It has a chimney, an ash pit, and a tuyere iron. The forced draft of air is blown through the tuyere iron from a centrifugal blower driven by an electric motor. The speed of the blower is controlled by a rheostat, and the air volume by a gate, similar to the damper vane in the old wood-fueled kitchen stove. The forge looks something like a stone fireplace (1).

The forge is cleaned completely; all dust, clinkers, and dirt must go. A clean fire is absolutely necessary if you intend to turn out consistently fine blades. As the man says, ''There's a hell of a difference between making horseshoes and turning out high-quality knife blades.''

The bladesmith must use a clean fire for forging, so the first job is to build a fire and make coke. Coke is the residue of coal when the gaseous impurities have been removed by heat. As a matter of fact, even the rough blacksmith doesn't burn ''green coal''; coke burns cleanly and provides much greater heat.

**(2) Kerosene is a safe,
quick way to start the
fire.**

The fire is started with kindling, shavings, or wadded-up paper and a dash of kerosene (and **never, ever** use gasoline) (2). When this small fire is going well, a couple of handfuls of pea-coal (small pieces of coal the size of a pea) are added. This small fire is built over the top of the tuyere iron, and at this stage we turn on the air very gently. Gradually more coal is added, and as the fire builds, more air, until finally we really pour on the coal, two or three buckets full. Make a little mountain over the tuyere iron and when the fire is burning well and breaking through, reduce the air. Let the pile burn slowly and heat the coal well. After ten or fifteen minutes, using a shovel, we turn the whole fire over, just like turning hash-brown potatoes (3). Let it burn and heat again, until the fire is breaking out all over the surface of the pile. Now turn off the air and sprinkle water all over the spread-out fire until it is completely killed.

(3) Turn the fire over.

The best of soft coal forms some clinkers; there is no way to avoid it. The bladesmith can't be continually digging around in his fire either. The safe way to handle this problem is to be constantly raking new coke into the center of the fire, and leveling the fire bed. The goal is to build and maintain a constant ''deep'' fire. This deep fire keeps a good layer of coke under your work at all times, protecting it against the attack of unburned oxygen which would result in oxidation. If you have been working for several hours the chances are that clinkers will be hindering the air flow and will need removal. However, even at this point your work will not have been ruined.

The beginning bladesmith has an advantage over the other knifemakers. He has access to a large supply of usable steel that will serve him well to learn with, at a very low price. Most salvage yards or scrap dealers have carbon steel suitable for the beginner. This material will not take the place of the fine pure stuff used by the master smiths, but at pennies a pound it will make useful knives.

In this shop, we deal with the **pure quill**, the best steel available for the bladesmith. After thirty years of forging, the grades used here are **Type 0-1** and **Type W-2**, which make the best forged blades, in our opinion.

If the forging fire is one of the most important elements in bladesmithing, the anvil must be considered the basic working tool. Anything that can be used to hammer the hot metal on can be called an anvil, but anything less than an adequate anvil as we know it will be a handicap. The London anvil has evolved over many years and will handle all the needs of the forging blacksmith, if he learns to use it well.

The familiar horned anvil can weigh as little as a pound or so, and as much as several hundred pounds, but for the bladesmith an anvil of 75 to 125 pounds is about right.

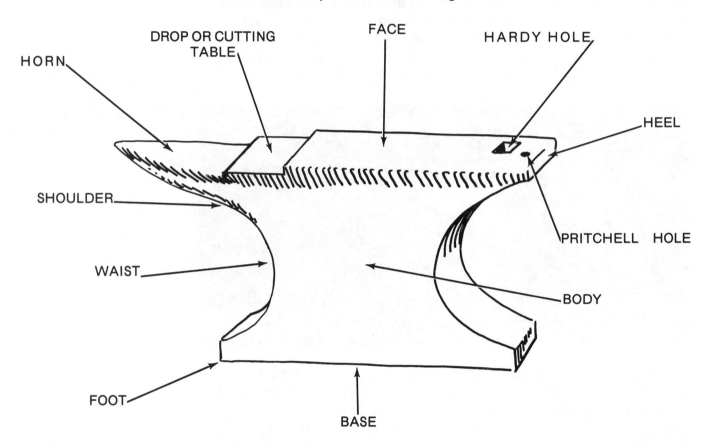

The best support for the anvil is a section of tree trunk about two feet in diameter, and set at least two feet into the earth floor of the shop. Merely setting the anvil on the tree trunk on a concrete floor is not good enough; you'll get too much bounce during heavy hammer work. When the anvil is set up, the working face should be about the height of your knuckles, when you are standing erect with your arms hanging loose. The anvil must be at the right working height to avoid strain on your arms and shoulders when working. The shock of heavy blows while forging is absorbed by the anvil and its support.

The best working floor around the forge and anvil is packed clay, or plain dirt. If your shop has a concrete floor, a four-foot square of dirt is best for the anvil area.

So far we've covered the fire and the anvil. Now we cover the third member of the triumvirate of basic bladesmithing tools, the hammer.

In this photo the most used hammer faces are shown (4). On the left is a square face with slightly rounded edges, known as the flatter. In the center is a single-jack, weighing 4 pounds. The hammer on the right is a modified single-jack shaped as a 45-degree cross peen on one end and as a straight peen on the other. Regular cross peen hammers can still be found for sale new, but not easily. Some smiths use a very heavy ball peen hammer for general work, and seem to do well with it. Except for small and delicate work, most hammers should weight at least 3 pounds. Most smiths have found that a 4 to 6 pound hammer is about right for heavy work.

Tongs are used to hold the hot steel, and they come in many sizes and shapes. And you won't be able to just go out and buy the kind you need. In most cases you'll have to learn how to make them yourself, as did the master smiths of old. Indeed, making the tools you will need will be a practical test of how you progress in the art of forging.

Note from the photos (5) the common tongs used here in this shop, and the different shapes of the gripping jaws (6). These tongs have been made especially for bladesmithing. Tong handles should be adjusted to lie about an inch or so apart when gripping the work. One of the best things that has happened to blacksmiths in years is the pliers known as **"Vise Grips,"** which can be adjusted to grip through a large range of parts and can be set to hold without constant pressure. These pliers are sold everywhere, and will be useful for holding all sorts of small work.

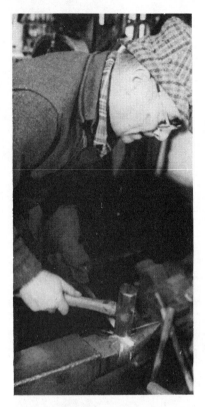

(8) Hammering the tang round.

(9) The hardy in place and in use.

Most of the knives made in the Moran shop are of narrow tang design. Experience has led us to believe that the best narrow tang construction starts with a stub tang on the blade and the rest of the tang, including the threaded end, is made from low carbon steel. The two are joined together, usually by arc welding or, rarely, by forge welding. The mild steel tang end offers great toughness and shock resistance.

These tang ends are made up, for most knives, of 1/4-inch x 1/2-inch bar stock about 18 inches long, giving us enough stock to hand-hold the work. Assuming that the fire is ready, we insert about 7 inches of the piece into the heart of the fire, raking coals around and over it. The air is turned on and regulated with the gate valve. Since this stock is rather thin, it will come to forging heat quickly and although the forging heat range isn't critical on mild steel, we keep a careful watch on the color, as a matter of habit. (See a good chart for the color range of 1800 to 1950 degrees F.)

When the temperature is right, take the stock from the fire. We are going to make a round shank about 3 inches long. First lay the heated bar against the horn of the anvil, and with light firm blows on first one edge of the bar and then the other, we establish the radius for the round portion of the tang. From this point, still working on the edges, we hammer toward the end in a series of blows, alternating edges with every blow. This is called drawing out (7). Whenever the heat drops below good forging temperature, we reheat, putting the stock back in the fire. Remember to close off the air when actually forging so as not to waste good coke.

At the point where the tang becomes square, move to the anvil face and put the tang against the flat. Working from the shoulder to the end, hammer it roughly round with short, rapid blows (8).

Now we cut the tang end to length. The stock is reheated to a bright red, and cut with a tool called a hardy cutter. Holding the stock in the left hand, we lay it across the hardy and strike with the hammer moderately, using as many blows as needed (9). We don't cut all the way through, because the hardy cutter and hammer would be damaged. Instead, after the stock cools slightly, a sharp rap on the edge of the anvil will complete the job.

(10) A square bar being drawn.

(11) **Special hammer for drawing and widening.**

(12) **The ''Little Giant'' power hammer.**

Now that the tang is ready, we'll start on the blade. Note from the photo (10) that we begin by forging a square stock into a wider and flatter bar using the special hammer with a half-round face (11). Note that the face is off axis. The other side of the hammer head looks the same except that it aligns with the handle. Held one way, the hammer forces the steel lengthwise; held the other way, it moves the steel at right angles to the bar. Note that the anvil horn is used in lengthening, and the face for widening.

And now is the time to meet the ''**Little Giant**'' power hammer (12), which in some shops is a very important piece of equipment. You'll note that the power hammer has a lower piece, called the anvil, mounted in place on the bed of the machine, and an upper moving piece, called the hammer, which moves vertically in fixed guides. This machine can be used to do the same work done by the hand hammer and the anvil horn, moving the hot steel as the smith wants it to go. Both the power hammer and the hand tools are used in the Moran shop; the power hammer can do in two heats what might take six or more heats with hand tools.

(13) **The drawing of steel with the ''Little Giant'' power hammer.**

(14) Steel at proper forging temperature cuts easy on the hardy.

(15) The easy tap separates the pieces.

(16) A "third hand" for the bladesmith.

But the end result is the same: a slightly too-thick bar, a bit shorter than the finished size of the knife blade. The excess must now be cut off, again on the hardy cutter (14). An easy tap or two, and the pieces are separated (15).

There's a third way to get to this point, and that is to use a piece of 1/4-inch flat stock of the required width, allowing for growth in the width and length from forging. Pictured here is a spring-powered device, called a "hold-down" (16). The stock is brought quickly from the forge to the anvil and placed under the hold-down. And right here you begin to realize the advantage of keeping your anvil warm; a cold anvil steals heat so fast as to make this work impossible.

Next we are going to cut the stub tang from this bar, using the age-old method. The blade blank is marked lightly with a chisel to indicate where to make the hot cut. The stock is brought hot from the forge and placed quickly under the hold-down. The hot cutter, held in the left hand, is placed on the chisel marks, and struck with the hammer (17). The result is a rough stub tang on the blade stock (18). After being trued up on the hard wheel grinder, the blade, along with the mild steel tang, is returned to the forge, where both are quickly brought up to forging heat and scarfed (19,20). The scarfed ends provide an overlap for the two pieces to be joined by forge welding. The two scarfed pieces to be joined are again heated, coated with a commercial welding flux (usually a mixture of borax and sal ammoniac) so that the flux completely coats the scarfed ends and then reheated to welding heat. These ends actually are slightly rounded, so that the first contact is made in the middle of the weld and subsequent blows will work any impurities or flux outward to the edges of the weld. The welding operation is one of the most difficult in bladesmithing, and only experience can train you to recognize the right heat for welding by eye alone.

(17) The "hot cutter" in position, the hammer falling.

(18) The stub tang as cut with the "hot cutter."

(19) The scarfing on the tang.

(20) The scarfing on the blade "stub tang."

(21) When cut nearly through...

(22) The knife point is shaped.

(23) Accurate hammer work comes from practice.

The next forging operations will take the blade to nearly the correct taper, outline, and thickness. We have described three ways to get to the bar of steel we now have: forging from bar stock, forging from smaller stock, and forging from mill-rolled stock. Normally the bar made by forging is carried through using forging methods, but the mill-rolled stock is sawed to rough outline on a metal-cutting bandsaw. Regardless of how the bar is obtained, the blade will be forged over the entire length.

When hand-forging the blade to outline, excess metal is removed with the hardy cutter while the steel is at forging temperature and the point is dressed up with the hammer at the same time. Hammer blows to both sides and top bring the point to a neat appearance (21). The particular design illustrated calls for an upswept point and the forging of the two sides moves the point higher and higher; the edge line becomes longer as a result of forging.

Forging must be done quickly, because the heat leaves the steel rapidly in thin sections such as knife blades. To work fast and accurately takes practice, a great deal of practice. Shown in the accompanying photos are some of the positions of blade, anvil, and hammer (22). Note that the hammer face must be precisely directed in bringing the edge down in thickness. While drawing the edge down, the back is struck to help maintain the correct curve (23). In the final photo the blade is shown laid lengthwise on the anvil face (24). No matter how carefully the blade is worked, it will want to bend, twist, or curve. The smith moves the steel around constantly, always correcting while molding. With the blade laid thus, the blows tend to straighten any curves to the right or left (25).

(24) The bladesmith's rhythm moves the growing blade form with a total unity.

72

The power hammer is the method of choice for those who pound hot steel for a living. It strikes fast and hard, or slow and gentle, at the direction of the operator.

(25) The kinks and curves are corrected with the blade in line with the anvil face.

The top hammer of the machine is the reverse of the anvil (25). Feeding the work from one direction elongates the steel bar; feeding it from the other direction widens and tapers it (26). The machine also controls the outline of the blade.

(26) In this position, the work is lengthened.

(27) The "Hammer" portion of the "Little Giant" power hammer.

We are now at a critical point in our forging operation. We must now "pack the steel." We uniformly heat the blade to the color of "sunrise red," or about 1100 degrees F. This is a hard color to judge visually; it helps to work in deep shadow or shade. After coming to the right color, the blade is brought to the anvil face and rapidly hammered or packed with a series of light blows, covering every bit of the surface. Care must be taken to work each side of the blade equally, with several trips back to the forge if needed.

When the blade forging is finished the steel will inevitably be warped or twisted at some point along its length. Now we put the bladesmith's fork to use. It is mounted in the hardy hole, the blade is inserted between the forks, and by carefully using the tongs, the blade is progressively straightened (27). It must be returned to the forge whenever it begins to cool down, and reheated as needed. Small areas of distortion should be corrected with the hammer.

Hopefully, we've finished this last step just about suppertime, because the next step is placing the blade in the fire and leaving it overnight to anneal. With what is left of the good fire, we heat the blade to a bright red and then lay it on the fire. The air is shut off and the blade completely covered with hot coals. As the fire dies down, the blade cools to room temperature, and by morning the steel is very soft, or annealed.

(28) The blade outline is ground true.

(29)Grinding leaves the edge with at least 1/16-inch thickness.

(30) The edge is constantly checked for straightness.

(31)The tang is ground to shape.

First the blade profile is trued up(28). Then the edge is ground leaving about 1/16th inch or so(29). Note that the edge bevel is at an angle of about 45 degrees(30). The edge must be sighted often during grinding to maintain straightness. The tang is also completely ground to size at this time(31).

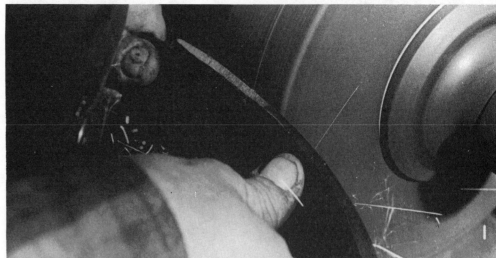

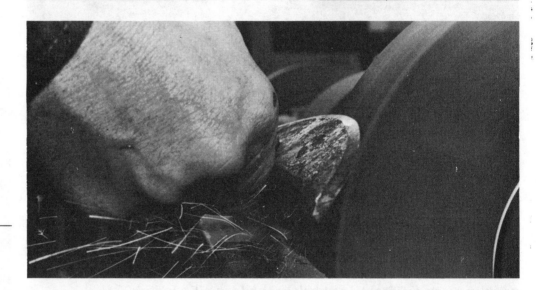

Three jobs remain to be done before going on to heat treatment. First, we must true up the shoulders that will back up the guard. Pictured is a special guide made up here, of two 5/16-inch x 1-inch steel bars at maximum hardness, with a spacer(32). The blade is inserted as shown, so that the shoulders are aligned with the guide bars.

The whole thing is clamped up in the vise, and the uneven portion of the blade shoulder is filed off, with the hardened bars keeping the file true(33). Note that a three-cornered file is used to finish up the acute angle next to the ricasso(34).

(32) The blade and filing guide clamped into vise.

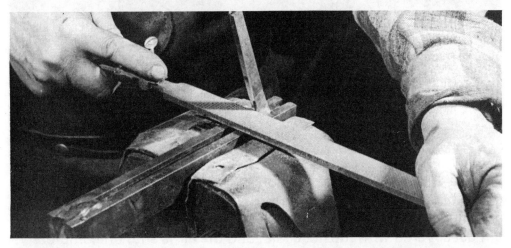

(33)The filing guide being used.

(34)The triangle file used for a tight spot.

Now the blade must be returned to the hard wheel grinder, and the rough surface smoothed up. The forging scale must be completely removed if it is not to retard the effect of the quench during heat treatment. Note that the grinding starts on the hard wheel, and is finished on the rubber contact wheel, using an abrasive belt. The forging scale is very hard, and it simply saves labor and belts if we start with the hard 36 grit wheel:

Now, we come to the heat treatment of our forged blade.

The forge is cleaned, and a good, fresh coke fire made up. When it is going well, it is raked level and a 1-inch rod of iron put in the fire and brought to red heat. While it is heating, a large old enameled coffee pot full of commercial tempering oil is placed next to the forge. A large thermometer is hung in the oil, and when the 1-inch rod is red hot, it is plunged into the oil, which begins to get hot very quickly. We remove the rod when the oil gets to 125-140 degrees F., which is the right temperature for quenching in this shop. Just before placing the blade in the soaking fire the oxy-acetylene torch is made ready.

(35) A loving look at a perfect color.

(36) The hot steel produces thick smoke.

Now, with a good hot fire going, we rake the fire, spreading it out flat and level. With the fire ready, the quenching oil warmed, and the torch set up, the blade is placed edge down in the fire. It is almost covered with the hot coals, and the air is shut off completely. Color begins to build slowly in the blade; we let the blade soak in the fire until it reaches a dull cherry red color (35); often quickly touching the heating blade with a magnet. Suddenly the magnet no longer goes to the steel; the blade has become non-magnetic. A moment or two longer in the slow-acting fire, and then the blade is plunged, point-first, down into the quenching oil, until the oil covers the entire blade but not the tang, which we want to stay soft. The action of the oil on the hot steel causes quite a lot of smoke above the quench pot (36), and as the smoke begins to dissipate, we remove the blade from the oil. It's just slightly too hot to hold in your bare hands, so we wrap our hands with heavy rags, and quickly take the blade to the hard wheel grinder, wiping off the excess oil just before grinding the blade bright again, all over (37).

As the blade comes out of the quenching oil, it is quite hard and brittle, and now it must be tempered.

With the blade ground bright and still quite warm, we light the oxy-acetylene torch, which has been set up with a #4 tip, and adjust the flame slightly rich, so there is a feather of paler blue fire beyond the bright inner hot cone. We start running the flame over the back of the blade, away from the cutting edge, keeping it moving always, pausing slightly over the heaviest areas around the ricasso and down the thick spine of the blade, back and forth, watching the color first come to a pale straw, then a dark straw, then through a reddish violet to finally a very light pale blue.

The purpose of this work with the torch is to draw the temper in the thickest part of the blade to a softer and tougher steel.

When you have the colors right, shut off the torch and return to the grinder; lightly grind the blade again until all traces of color are removed.

At this point we have a well-shaped blade, heat-treated and tempered, and ready for the further work of finishing and assembly.

To test for cracks which might have occurred during quenching, the blade is gripped by the tang, cutting edge up, and the back struck smartly against the horn of the anvil, with great force(38). Any hairline quench cracks in the steel will fracture at this point, due to the induced resonant vibrations from the blow. While striking the anvil, the bladesmith is also listening for that tell-tale "flat" sound that discloses a cracked structure.

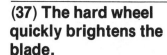

(37) The hard wheel quickly brightens the blade.

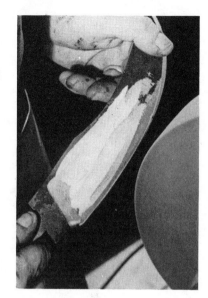

(38)Testing for a cracked blade.

Another test: about an inch of the point of the blade is clamped up in the bench vise, using soft jaws. The tang is pushed sideways, with moderate force, enough to deflect the blade about 10 degrees(39). When the blade survives this, only one test remains; a new file is pushed across the cutting edge area of the blade. It should almost bite, and almost slip, showing that the edge is in optimum condition for finishing.

Now the blade goes to the Square Wheel grinder, set up with an 8-inch rubber contact wheel, running a new 60 grit belt. We completely re-grind the blade to finished size and final shape. After the 60 grit work, we change belts, going now to a 220 grit belt, and

(39)Testing for a brittle blade.

(40) Angle grinding for blade flatness and finish.

working at right angles to the 60 grit lines (40), we re-grind completely with the finer belt, sighting along the cutting edge frequently to keep it true and straight. As we progress with the 220 grit belt, low spots in the finish will show up readily, noticeable by the deeper 60 grit scratches from the previous work with the coarse belt. These low spots require that the rest of the flat be brought down to meet them.

When you have a smooth, true surface on both sides of the blade, you are ready for the next step: we change belts again, and this time go to a very fine 500 grit finishing belt for the last grinding operation. Again, working at an almost right angle to the 220 scratches, we completely go over the blade, this time paying special attention to the area of the ricasso and being careful not to take off too much (41).

(41) Fine grinding the ricasso.

The next step is buffing the blade. In this shop, it is done on 12-inch diameter wheels, and the buffer is driven by a 5-horsepower motor. And right here we are going to stop a moment and talk about safety.

There is no single operation in knifemaking so hazardous as buffing. Pay attention to this job, because if you get just a little careless, parts of the knifemaker can end up on the shop floor. That may sound ugly, and in fact we mean it just that way. The beginning worker should practice on round stock with no sharp edges to catch the wheel. Even then, be careful when you work up the ends. And when you are ready to work on an actual blade get your head screwed on right, allow no distractions whatever, and lock the shop door so no visitor can walk in unannounced and startle you. Then give the work your complete and undivided attention.

(42) The big wheel buffer in action.

The initial buffing is done with a large puckered buff, charged with a ''cut and color'' compound, and removes most of the scratches left by the grinding belt. As with the grinding, we cover the entire blade moving in one direction, and then go over the work moving at right angles to it, so as to show up any imperfections in the basic finish(42).

(43)Lungs and eyes need constant protection in many operations.

All this buffing work must be done while wearing a breathing mask, or respirator, and safety glasses or goggles(43). The moving buffing wheel fills the air around the job with very fine lint; the buffing compound also sometimes gases off during the heat of buffing, and none of this is very beneficial. So protect yourself—nobody else is going to do it for you.

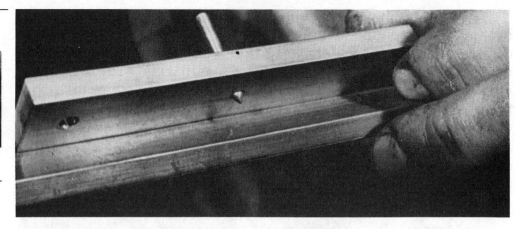

(44) Marking gauge for guard.

(45) Gauge indicates length and center.

(46) The Whitney punch machine.

(47) The hole in the guard made by the punch.

When the basic finish has been refined on both sides of the blade, we are ready to make the guard. We mark off the center, punch it, scribe the line for length (44,45) and then take the brass bar to a bench-mounted **#20-1 Whitney Punch,** where we punch the rectangular hole for the tang (46,47). Next, the guard is sawed from the brass bar stock and shaped up, first on the square wheel and then on a smaller belt sander. It is then polished on a **Baldor High Speed Buffing Lathe** with a cotton buff (48).

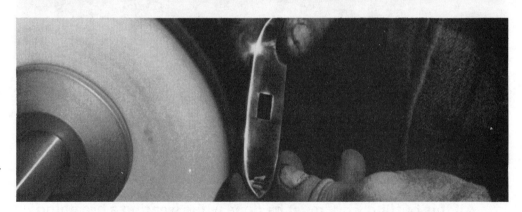

(48) As always, use caution with the buffer.

The guard is made to fit tightly so that the last fit is a "drive" fit.

The guard is then soldered to the blade—nothing fancy, just soft solder. It keeps moisture out of the joint. The solder is applied from the bottom and drawn up through the guard-blade joint.

80

Our attention is now turned to the handle. A piece of well-dried curly maple is selected. A handle pattern is laid over the wood and a line traced with a pencil (49). The plank of maple is taken to a wood cutting bandsaw, and the outline of the handle is sawed (50). The ends are squared up on a combination horizontal band sander and disk (51).

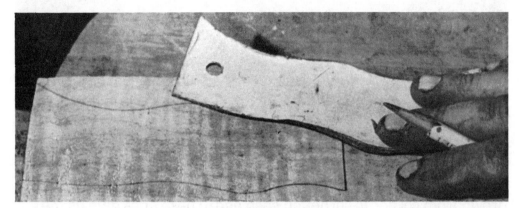

(49) The lines of the handle.

(50) The bandsaw following guide lines.

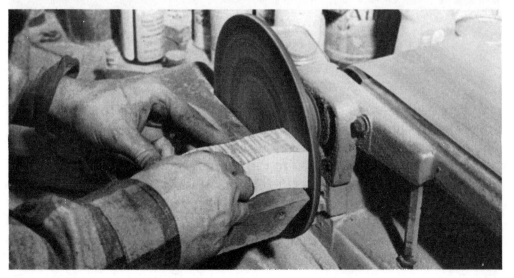

(51) Squaring the handle block.

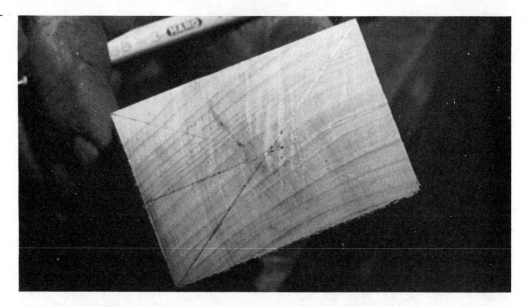

(52) Center locating lines on ends of the handle stock.

The profiled handle blank is taken to the bench and lines are drawn from corner to corner on each end. These lines give us the centers(52). The blade is laid along the blank(53), the guard snug against the wood, and the line for the tang end hole is established(54).Now we move to the drill press.

(53)The tang is laid along the handle for hole location.

(54) The location of the true tang hole.

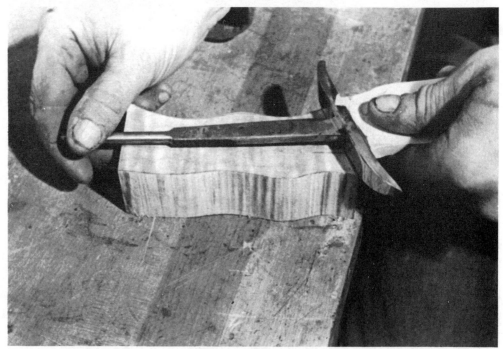

(55) Drill and pointed locating pin.

The drill press is set for drilling the handle. Note that the brad point centers on the steel point bolted to the drill press table(55). The centers are marked, one end of the handle wood is placed on the point, and the drill is lowered to the upper point. This assures that the hole through the handle stock is exactly where we want it. The hole is drilled. Now the back of the handle can be sawed to the final angle(56). Incidentally, the block was left with parallel ends until this stage for easier handling. The newly-sawed end is trued on the sanding disk(57) and the way is clear to move on.

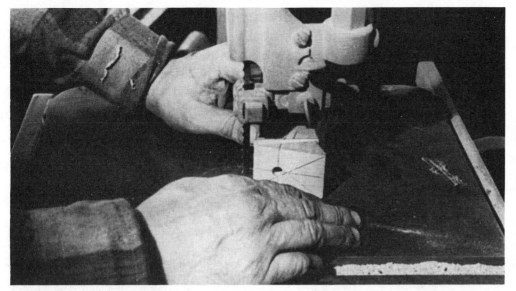

(57)Squaring the handle faces.

The tang of the knife is rectangular and the hole through the handle is round. Clamping up the wood in the vise, we use a modified rasp to elongate the hole(58) . To be sure that the fit will be snug, check the tang frequently. Note from the picture that the blade has been wrapped in masking tape, for protection of both the blade and the maker(59).

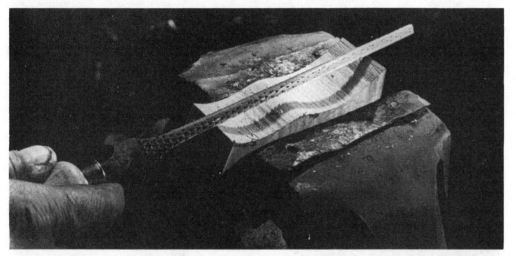

(58) The modified rasp.

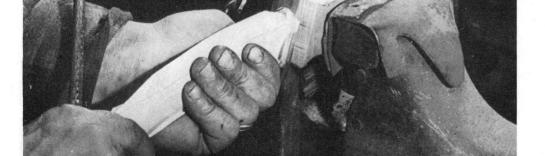

(59)First trial fitting.

When the handle fits nicely against the guard, we turn to the butt cap. A pattern is clamped up on the brass bar stock and scribed(60). The butt cap is sawed and taken to the metal cutting bandsaw and trimmed(61). Now the brass cap and the block are clamped securely in the vise and hit with the hammer. The cap is then set against the tang and scribed to locate the hole that will be drilled.

(60) The butt cap pattern in use.

(61) The brass stock is sawed to the guide lines.

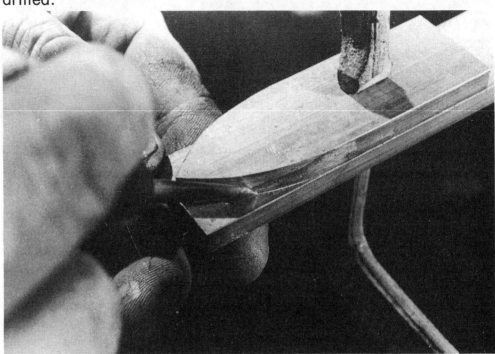

We take a minute to thread the tang. Find the right brass nut and try the complete handle on for size. While the handle is on the blade and lined up properly, we mark the junction between the guard and hand material (62).

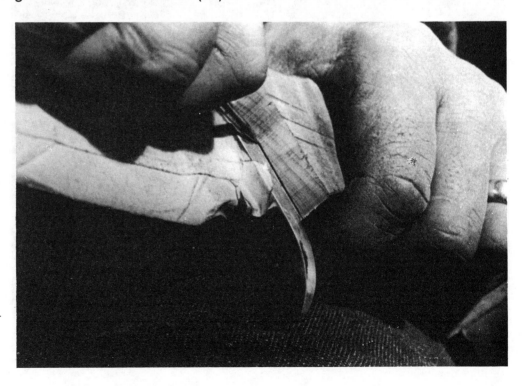

(62) Lines are marked and handle will be ground down to them.

84

The knife is then disassembled and we take the handle to the grinder. The platen attachment is put on in place of the large wheel. Running a new 60 grit belt, we start working on the handle(63).

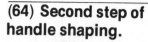
(63) **Beginning the handle shaping.**

(64) **Second step of handle shaping.**

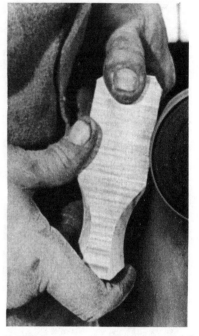

Running the 3-inch wheel (the larger wheel on the platen attachment), the first heavy sanding of the handle is to the marks we made on the wood where it joins the guard. Both sides are ground equally. The small wheel grinds a radius just back of the guard area. Then another radius is ground behind the first. Next the work is transferred to the smaller machine with the very soft 3-inch wheel and a finer grit belt, where smoothing continues(64,65).

(65) **The smaller belt sanding machine continues the sanding and blending.**

(66) Excess brass is sawed free.

(67) Tang is sawed even with the nut.

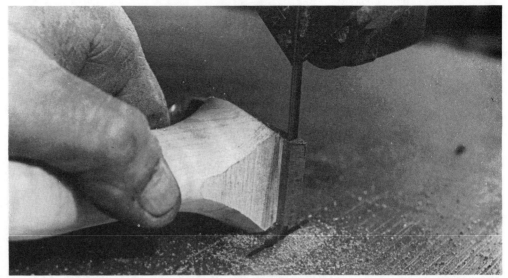

Next we assemble the handle again, this time to blend wood to brass. The butt is put on behind the wood, a nut run down and tightened, and the knife is taken to the metal-cutting bandsaw where the excess brass is sawed free(66). The tang is trimmed to the nut at the same time (67).

The knife is returned to the 3-inch wheel and now the brass and wood are worked together. When the rougher work is done, the knife is taken to the smaller machine and both brass and wood are further smoothed and blended.

The curly maple is progressively sanded with open coat abrasive paper, from 220 grit size to the eventual 500 grit finish.

The knife is clamped up in a drill press vise and that in turn is clamped to a heavy mechanic's vise (68). The round file is used with firmness but with attention(69). Small half-round grooves are spaced from one end of the guard to the other. The little knife-edge file is used to cut a neat straight line between the grooves. The butt cap is handled the same way(70).

(68)Filing decorative grooves in the guard.

(69) The grooves are equally deep and evenly spaced.

86

Next the high-speed **Baldor** buffer with a charged cotton wheel quickly removes the scratches left by the files. Care must be taken with small pieces; the buff will snatch and throw them with great force.

After a quick final sanding, it's time to apply the water dye. The brown dye makes the grain pattern of the curly maple change from a rather plain looking wood to a dramatic patterned handle (71,72). The dye penetrates the wood—deeper than an oil-based dye would go. The finish on the handle is now given its final sanding, but with a twist. The handle is wetted with a tissue soaked in plain water, then briefly held inside the coal stove where it picks up heat very quickly. This procedure raises the grain of the wood. That grain is lightly sanded smooth with 500 grit paper, and the sequence is repeated until no grain rises.

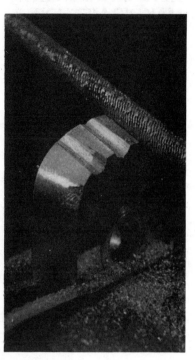

(70) The techniques used on the guard are used on the butt cap.

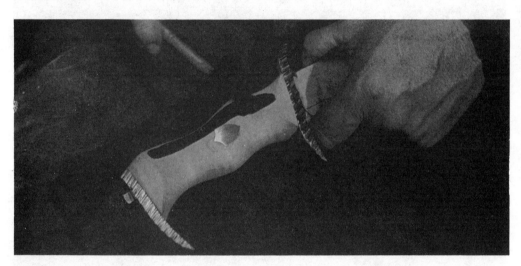

(71, 72) The water dye works wonders.

Now raw linseed oil is generously applied. The wood soaks it up rapidly. Subsequent coats are given until the wood will accept no more. This may take a period of a week or so. The handle now is finished except for buffing with a clean buff.

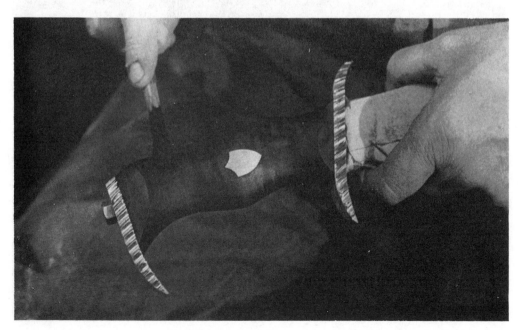

ALTERNATE SHEATH-MAKING METHOD

The leather used in Moran's sheaths is a fine 8- to 10-ounce strap grade dyed leather purchased by the hide.

(1) The "Head Knife," an old, old tool still used today.

The leather is cut to width with a very old strap cutter made of steel, iron and brass. It operates as shown. The leather is cut to length with what is called a "head cutter" or "head knife" (1). The blade and guard are laid on a length of leather and marked (2). Another line is made for the seam and the leather is cut to the outside lines (3). This section will become the front of the sheath.

(2) The pattern as traced.

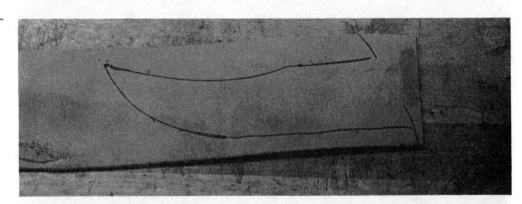

(3) The welt line is drawn now.

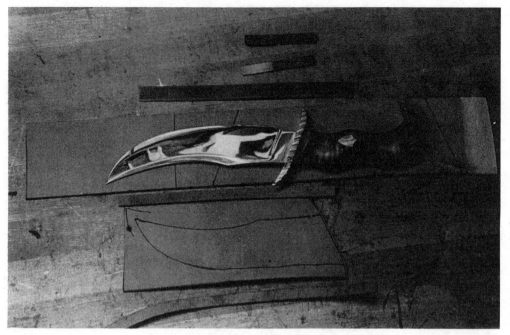

(4) The sheath parts.

(5) A neat job, a simple tool.

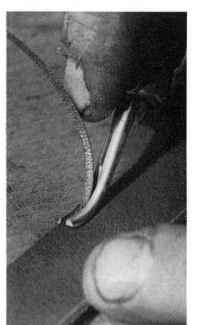

The back of the sheath is cut out next, allowing for the belt loop and a generous fold-back. This is cut to length and the fold-back part skived. The keeper strap, the welts, and the spacers are cut to length (4). The keeper strap is rounded on the edges with a leather edger (5). Now the glue is applied to those parts, the first to be joined (6,7). This contact cement is left to dry to the touch before gluing up. The strips that are to become the welt are carefully applied (8) and then, when firmly pressed down, the front is trimmed to size (9).

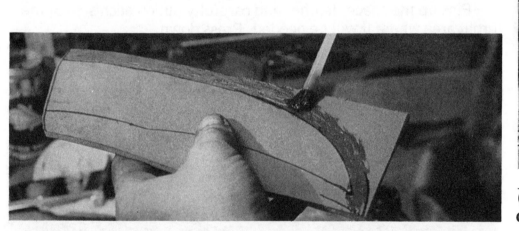

(6,7) Be generous with cement, not sloppy.

(8) Take care that the first effort is right.

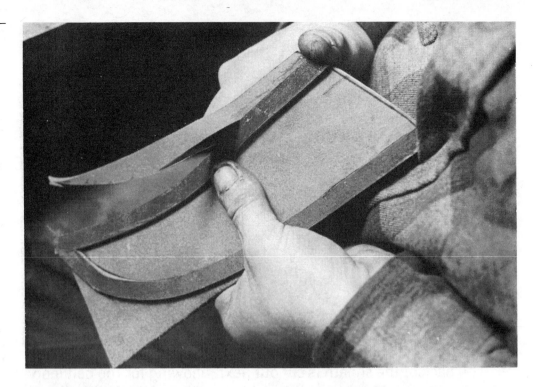

Now is the time to attach the bottom half of the snap to the sheath front.

The back and the belt loops are next. Use the top half for the pattern and mark around the blade(10). Next, apply cement to both sides of the spacer leather and set on edge to dry. Apply cement to the welt and to the keeper strap where it will be incorporated into the body of the sheath. Yes, skive an inch or two of that also.

Pick up the spacer leather and carefully put on each side of the throat area where it will be needed. Press down.

Now for the keeper strap; be sure that it's going to come out with the finished side up. Put it into position and press firmly down(11). (Note in the same picture that the back has been coated with cement too.)

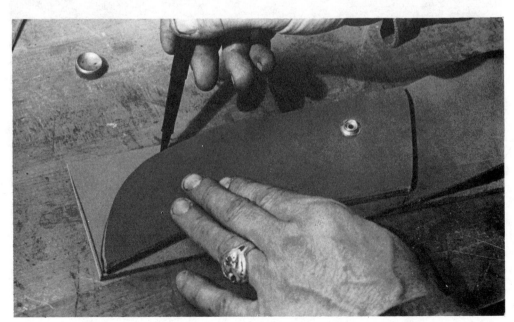

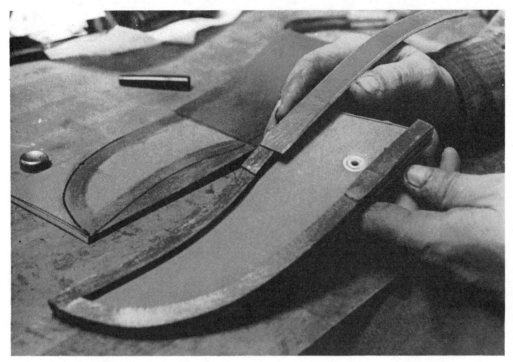

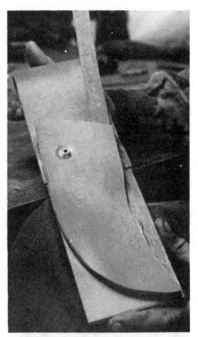

(11)The keeper becomes one with the sheath.

Check all surfaces to be joined for a good coating of cement. Apply some to the keeper strap as needed. When everything is set up good and dry to the touch, carefully put the two halves of the sheath together(12).

Now slip the blade into the sheath. It should be a tight fit. Trace around the handle(13), leaving some space on each side. Remove the knife and very carefuly trim the sheath to size. Cut along the knife sheath front, along the handle line, and on around the knife (14).

Next a sharp new belt with 220 grit is wound on the grinder and the whole sheath edge is trimmed up(15).

(12)Carefully, carefully.

(13)Draw a line around the handle leaving good clearance.

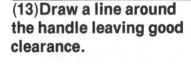

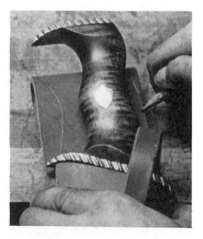

(14)Trim around the sheath.

(15)Keep the sheath at right angles to the wheel.

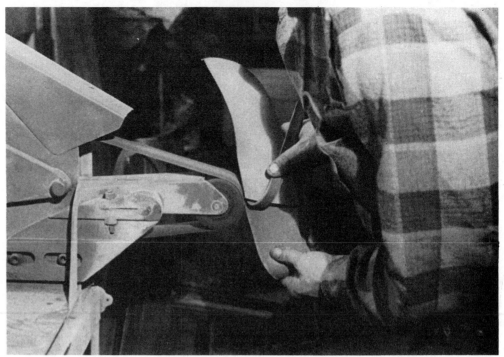

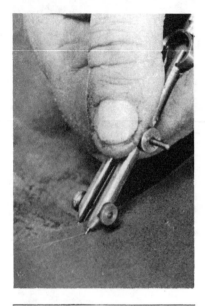

(16)A light or heavy mark is o.k.

(17)Another important but inexpensive tool.

Back at the bench, dividers are used to scribe a line around the blade portion of the sheath that will be the guide for stitching(16). The stitch spacer(17) now is used firmly to establish the marks for the thread holes.

Anyone who has tried to force a sewing awl through a couple of layers of tough 10-ounce leather will appreciate the problems in putting a true hole through six thicknesses. There are two solutions: (A) purchase the best single-stitch machine money can buy; or, (B) put the drill press to work. The drill press just happens to be basic to knifemaking, and one of the reasons it enjoys that importance is the many varied jobs it can do. Right now, it is going to work as a hole maker in leather. A long tapered needle is made of 1/8 drill rod. To operate, chuck up the needle, place a paper towel on the drill press table to keep the leather clean, put the sheath face up on the towel, line up the needle and the hole and turn on the machine. Now you just "drill" the holes, all of them(18).

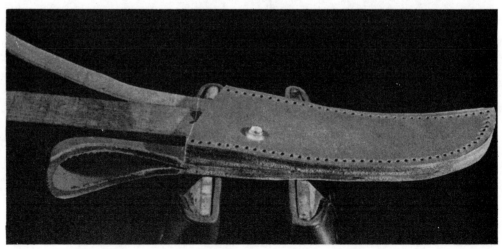

(18)Neat holes, equally spaced.

Now a length of heavy linen thread is cut from the spool. Hopefully, you can measure in your mind enough to do the whole sewing job without splicing. A thick sheath such as we are making takes a surprising amount—as much as twelve feet of thread. This is a problem but is better than trying to cover up a splice. The ends of the thread are fished through the eyes of two stout needles. It pays to put wax on both of your thumbs and first fingers so that you can pull the needles with more of a grip. One needle is poked through the first hole in one direction and the other is pushed through the same hole in the opposite direction. The slack is taken up and the thread is pulled as tight as you can(19,20). Continue this until complete. The finish stitch is doubled back a couple of holes and the thread is cut close to the leather.

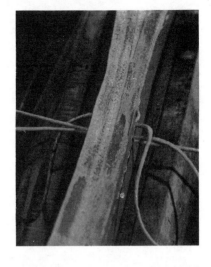

(19)At first, there is a lot of thread to pull.

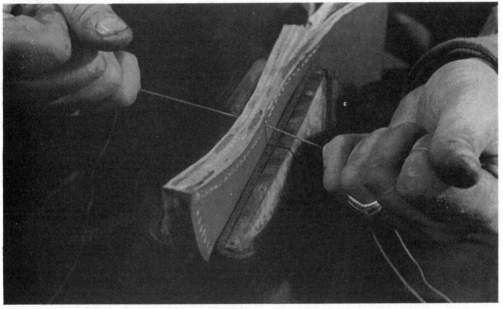

(20)This can be a little hard on soft hands.

Then the sheath is taken to the belt grinder and lightly trued again. Next the sheath is taken to the bench, where all the sharp edges are trimmed with the edging tool.

We go next to the buffer. A special wheel, made of hardwood (lignum vitae) and polished, is put on the arbor. The face of the wheel is coated with wax. The machine is turned on and the edges of the sheath are burnished(21).

All that is left is to install the other half of the snap on the keeper strap. The knife is put into the sheath and the keeper strap is pulled tight across the bottom snap, centered, and pressure is applied so that an impression is made on the bottom of the keeper strap. Punch the hole out and fasten the snap to the strap.

All that is used for finish in this shop is a liberal coat of high quality shoe wax of the correct color, rubbed in well, followed by another coat that is rubbed well and polished.

It's all done but the final buffing of the blade with green chrome polish. Oh yes, little spots here and there may need a touch-up. But your knife is finally finished, the fire is out, and it's time for a rest and a wee bit of the water of life.

(21)Working the edges with the wooden wheel at high speed.

HOW TO MAKE A KNIFE WITH HAND TOOLS

(A Special Effort By Richard R. Barney)

Although the method is impractical, a knife can be made using hand tools alone. As we proceed, the reader will recognize ways he can use any power tools he may have, and will probably use them. For instance, those who have a little electric drill will be tempted to use it. The same would apply to those who have some sort of power grinder. Some of us take a particular delight in doing things the hard way; our pleasure comes from meeting just such a challenge.

The steel for our blade will be simple oil-hardening 0-1. It is easier to work than most other tool steels, and is widely available in surfaced stock in many sizes. We have chosen 3/16-inch by 1-1/4 inches, and the piece was 18 inches long. These dimensions will allow us freedom in design and a thick enough blade for heavy use.

Among the tools we will need are at least four types of files. The main working files are big, bigger than you may think are necessary. But the reason is to gain pressure on the work: the length allows us to really bear down with a lot of body weight. The two flat files are 14 inches long, and so is the square file. One of the flat files is called a "second cut" and the other is a "nu-cut smooth." They are about 1-3/8 inches wide and have a double-cut pattern. The square file is about 5/8-inch wide on its flats and has four working sides. The fourth file is called a "cant" file and its use will be described later.

The wide files will be used to keep the flats of the blade truly flat. The long, narrow square file, with its coarse teeth, will be used for the initial heavy stock removal. This file allows maximum pressure to be put on the steel bar, and it hogs off the steel with pleasing speed. Other files will be introduced later as the need arises.

You need a hacksaw, a stout one with a rigid frame, and some good quality hacksaw blades. This tool gets rid of unwanted steel much faster than trying to file it off.

There are all kinds of hand drills. The kind we will use is a brace and bit type, with a twist drill used in place of the wood bit more commonly used with this tool.

Abrasive paper is a working tool in this kind of knifemaking. It's the same stuff that is sold in auto supply houses in various grit sizes.

Now all of these tools work. With your body as a power source, they work. But they only work well if the knife steel is held firmly—really solid. Shown in most of these pictures is a very old vise variously called a "leg" or "post" vise. It was used mostly for heavy-duty work and is very strong. It, too, must be held securely, and that means some sort of bench that won't move under the kinds of pressure we are going to apply.

Now the thinking man is going to give a lot of thought to the design of this blade. The thought that the steel is going to be removed by hand gives a completely different slant to design concepts. It is not practical to try for any kind of hollow grind: it could be done, but at a price just too high. So the blade will be flat ground, wedge-shaped, and the width will be measured in sore

1
FULL TANG

2
NARROW TANG

3
HENRY STYLE RABBET TANG

4
BLIND TANG

5
JAPANESE TANG

(Drawing #1)The major variations in mounting the handle.

muscles. How will the handle be attached to the blade? There are all sorts of ways, (drawing #1) the full tang, the hidden tang, etc. In the sketch, numbers 3 and 5 have handles made of two halves, with space rabbeted out of each half so that when the halves are joined, there is a tang hole that matches the tang exactly.

In keeping with this project, we think it's appropriate to go to the hidden or narrow tang kind of handle construction. This style seems more traditional, it's an old concept, and it fits the idea of making a knife by hand.

To lessen the work, we decided to make a blade that can fall loosely into the category of "general utility." The whole knife will be about 8-1/4 inches long with a handle that will be about 4-1/8 inches long. We have some 1/4-inch brass on hand, so that will become the guard.

The simple way to lay out a blade on paper is shown (1). We use the steel for the width and lay out the blade length, the guard and the handle with common drawing tools (2).

(1)Lay the steel stock on the pattern paper and trace the lines that define the knife's width.

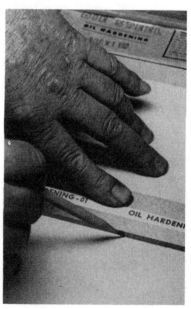

(2)Locate the position of the guard.

(3) Note the areas allotted to blade, guard, and handle.

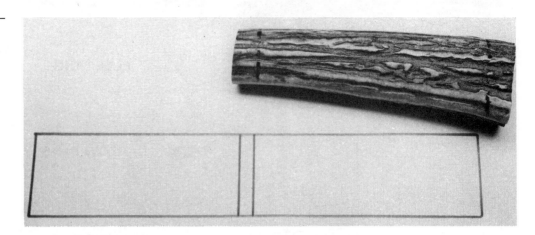

Now one of the reasons for the narrow tang choice is the piece of stag (3). It's a nice-shaped section from Bob Schrimsher's knife supply house in Texas. The blade design (4) is simple. Note that in the picture the tang is curved, while in the lay-out pattern (5) the tang is straight. We have to saw out the tang portion, and the saw only cuts in straight lines. The tang will be curved later.

(4) The completed pattern . . . . .

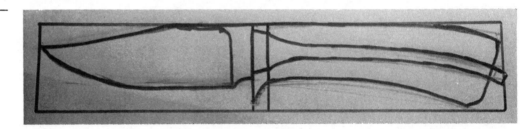

(5) Ready to cut out.

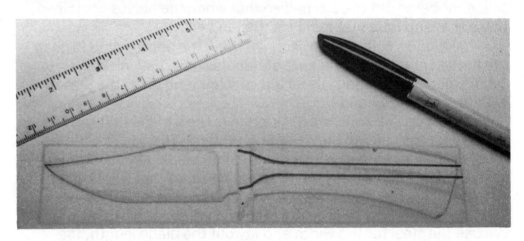

There are many ways to transfer a pattern from lay-out paper to something more substantial, but this is an easy way. Cut the pattern out, leaving plenty of space around it. Then spray with an adhesive, using newspaper to protect the table surface. The actual pattern is a fiber material that is widely used by knifemakers for spacers and slab handle liners. Just smooth the paper on top of the liner material, and then cut out the main portions with sharp shears (6). The more delicate portions of the pattern are cut with a sharp knife (7), and you end up with a firm pattern that can be used many times (8).

(7) And a sharp knife for the tight spots.

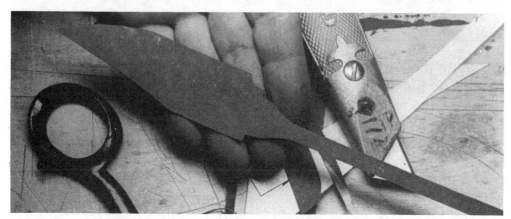

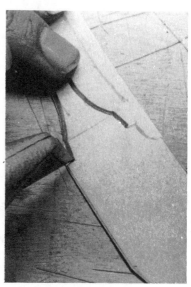

(8) The finished pattern ready to transfer to steel.

The beautiful steel finish on this ground stock, 0-1, has the lines of the grinding running along the length of the bar, and this makes it very difficult to see a scribed line. We fix that by coating the steel with a quick-drying dye called "lay-out blue." This coating dries rapidly and when a line is cut through it with a scribe it is very easy to see (9).

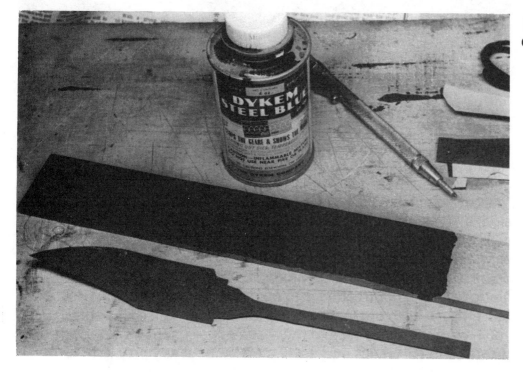

(9) The steel should be coated with lay-out dye.

(10) Scribe a heavy line around your pattern.

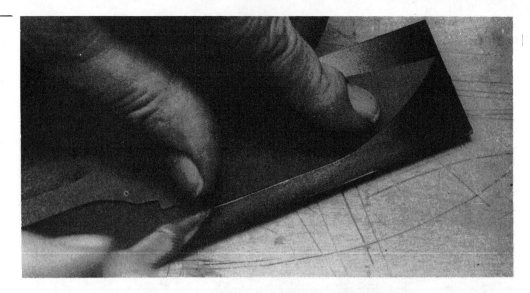

With the pattern ready and the **Dykem steel blue** dry, lay the pattern on the steel, hold it steady with one hand, and scribe an accurate line around the pattern (10). Be particular about the shoulders of the blade, that area that the guard will butt against.

We haven't yet mentioned what should be done with the butt end. This has been more or less settled, because the stag has a pithy center and must be covered. The angle of the butt is therefore, established, and we will have to have a butt cap. By threading the tang for an inch or more, we can leave our options open for now.

(11) Keep work clamped up close.

(12) And then begin cutting out the blade.

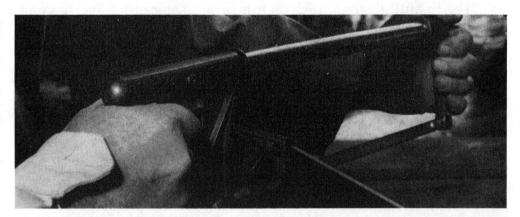

Notice in the photo how close the bar is positioned to the jaws of the vise. This is a rule that must be learned both in sawing and filing. Keep the work clamped up close; and move the work whenever the distance from the jaws to the cut of the filing surface gets more than 1/2- to 3/4-inch away. This is shown in the photo (11). The cut was started at the top; and each time the slightest sign of vibration appeared, the steel was moved so that the cut was near the vise jaws. Now the hacksaw will only cut so deep, and some short cuts must be made to accommodate this limitation (12). Some of the cuts will start at an angle. The only way to get the saw going in the right direction is to begin to cut in the wrong direction. Start the cut with the teeth turned toward the bulk of the steel, until you have a little step to hold the blade edge. Then turn the edge in the direction of choice and it will start without any problem (13).

(13) Turn the hacksaw.

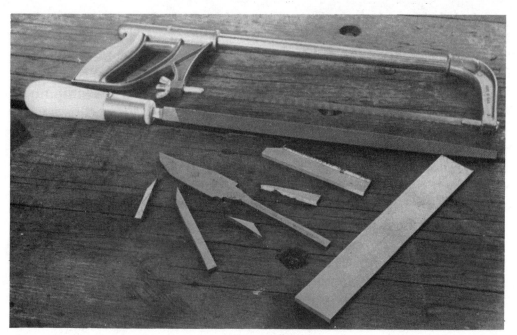

(14) Ready for cleaning up with the files.

Getting the rough outline is just a matter of sawing away everything possible without worrying too much about details. Just be sure to stay on the outside of the scribed lines. When you are through, you'll end up with something like this (14).

Now let's meet the half round file (15). It is used for curved surfaces as shown. Even though it doesn't exactly match the radius of this curve, moving the file slightly along the steel while filing across the edge will produce just what you want. You have to watch what is happening all of the time, of course. The small flat file is called a Swiss pattern flat file(16); it must be used here because the larger file is just too wide and would cut into the tang where we don't want any cuts.

The narrow part of the tang is clamped up tight in the vise (17) and we file true to the line.

(15) Clean up these areas carefully.

(16) Using the Swiss pattern flat file.

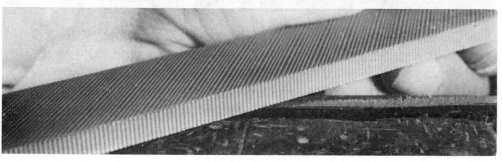

(17) Clamp the work down in the vise, and file away.

99

(18)Take care filing guard–shoulder joint.

(19,20)A homemade scriber.

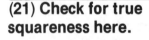

(21) Check for true squareness here.

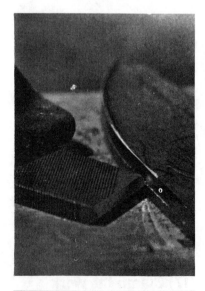

(22) Scribe the cutting edge guide lines.

In this kind of blade design, there is a critical area that must be right if the knife is going to look professional. This is where the guard butts against the shoulders of the blade. It must be filed with great care(18). In addition, the guard and shoulders must be lined up. The way that has been accomplished here is by clamping a short piece of straight steel scrap to the blade with Vise Grips and scribing a line across the ricasso. Notice that the scribe(19,20) is made from an old rat-tail file that has been carefully ground to a very sharp point—without heating, by the way. It works well, and only requires that you know someone with a grinder. A special note: cultivate this friend with the grinder, as you will need that grinder later. In practice, that scribed line need not extend across the ricasso as it is just one more scratch that has to be removed. In Section II, Chapter 3, ''Making A Knife At The Moran Forge,'' a device is shown for filing these shoulders exactly right. If you plan to make a few knives, learn this method(21) of checking the shoulders for squareness.

Our next need is a line that will show exactly where the centerline of the blade will be (22). We will use an old flat file that has been ground to a ''V,'' with the edge the right height. As seen, it is clamped to a flat piece of scrap hardwood, and then the blade is drawn along this edge. In this instance, a line is scribed along the top of the blade because we are going to do a ''trick'' thing there after a while.

The transition line from blade to ricasso is marked out (23) with a marking pen. Now, back to that scrap of steel used as a scribe guide. This time, it becomes a file guide. It is clamped up with the Vise Grips so that the edge corresponds with the line we have just drawn. Use a scrap of leather on the underside of the steel because that area is the ricasso and we don't want to mar the surface. The file shown (24) is a square taper file with one "safe" side. Drawing #2 shows the principle of the safe side file. There are many types, sizes and designs of files with this feature. We will be using them often. Observe the sizes and applications so that you can order some that are right for the job.

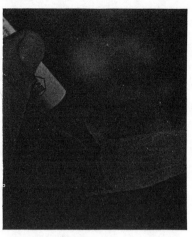

(23) Roughly mark where your bevel stops.

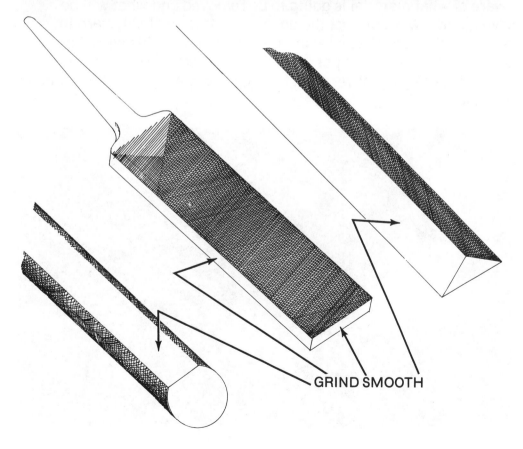

(24) The filing guide is clamped in place.

GRIND SMOOTH

(Drawing #2)You'll have to make your own safe edge files from standard ones.

Placing the safe or smooth side of the file against the guide, file a groove down almost to the line that marks the center of the blade edge (25). This groove can reach from the edge to near the back of the blade, but leave some untouched steel near the back for insurance. Do this to both sides.

(25) To control the bevel location.

We are going to taper the blade from the point to about the midway part of the blade. Right here, another important "tool" is introduced. It is a 1/4-inch piece of bar stock. One end is clamped very tightly in the jaws of the vise and the remainder becomes a holding device for our filing. Notice that we use two Vise Grips here to reduce any vibration. Take a look at the Vise Grip near the point. There is nothing beneath the serrated jaws to protect the steel. This is simply because that steel will come off later. Always be aware of what material is going to be removed and what will be saved, and always protect the good stuff. It is devilishly hard to remove deep scratches later on. Using the big flat file with the coarse teeth, we file a taper in the blade. There are two sets of centerlines as guides: we must try to produce a taper that is equal on both sides.

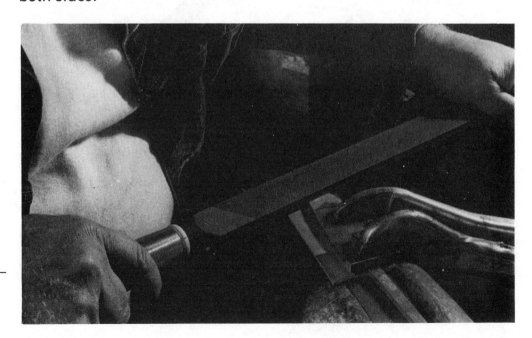

(26) Be careful with this big brute; it cuts fast and deep.

Before we pick up that big square file, here are some pointers on filing.Careless or uncontrolled filing case cause lots of problems. For instance, the back of the blade is a nice, finished piece of steel. A few mistakes there with the file, and the back is scarred and will have to be refinished. No big deal? Consider that the blade that we are making is flat ground from edge to back. To correct a deep scratch in the back means taking off enough steel to leave a nice, even smooth finish—all the way from back to edge! What is more, to do it right, the OTHER side of the blade must be equally filed. It's far easier to be careful(26).

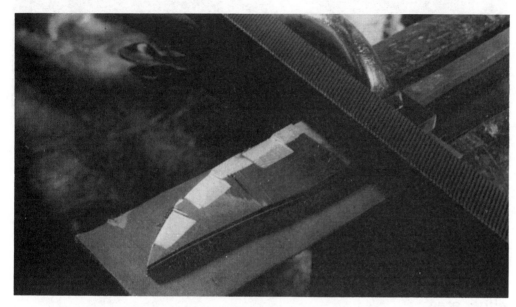

(27) **File grooves almost to the centerline; not too close.**

In the beginning stages, it might be a good idea to fold tape over the back of the blade so that you can tell when the danger area is being marked. At least it will only tear at the tape, and will help you get used to the idea of accurate filing. Your hands must learn how to file with a great deal of downward pressure. At the start, you must lower your head and see how the file lays on the work. Set it right on the steel to start, and then try to maintain that angle while filing. Keep checking until you know where the file is at all times.

At times, you can use the marks left by the filing strokes as a guide. At other times, there is no room for mistakes and you'll have to set the angle of the file by eye.

Now go back to that big square file (27). In the picture it might appear that we are filing right against the steel guide. But the file is just resting there. Note the square grooves filed near the edge: these grooves are filed **near** the centerline but not **to** it. The reason for the staggered grooves is twofold: one, it takes off lots of metal in a short time, and two, these grooves serve as guides for the flat filing to come.

After this filing has been done on both sides, take the big flat file and start filing away all that unwanted steel. These big files seem to have minds of their own and sometimes they cut smooth the first try. But sometimes you have to change the angle of filing strokes until you find the one angle that works best. File away until

(28) Change angles while filing until it looks like this.

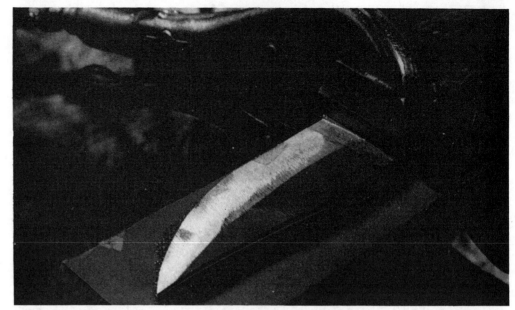

(29) Mark areas to be filed.

you have something that looks like this photo(28). Do both sides. Note: Do you see that block of steel still clamped to the blade? That is the best insurance possible. It prevents any stray filing strokes from rampaging into that ricasso area and messing up the looks of the blade forever.

The filing of the flat blade has now progressed to a little over half way to the back, and must continue. We mark both the edge of the blade and the back with a black marking pen(29). This is more good cheap insurance, for it instantly shows if the file is biting into either area.

(30) Draw file the false edge.

You may now switch to the big file with the finer teeth. And file away, file away. File over the surface in one direction and then file in another. This gives you visual reference to just what is being removed at the time. If those marks don't show all, draw file the whole thing(30) and that will help. Be sure to let the files cut nearly in line with the blade at times: this will help keep everything flat and true.

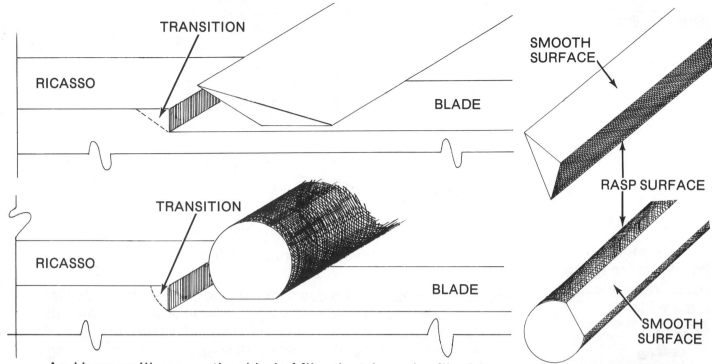

And here we'll use another kind of file, the triangular file. More properly, this one is known as a "cant" file. This is an expensive file that only does a tiny bit. Drawing #3 shows how we prepare the cant file and what it does to the transition from edge to ricasso. Check the photo(31). I suppose that a square angle there wouldn't harm the way the knife works, but it looks much better with some angle to it. If you don't like the kind of angle the triangular cant file makes, the drawing also shows the way to prepare a round file to do the same kind of job. (This presupposes that you are still friends with the man who has the grinder.) Whichever file you choose, file very carefully, making sure that the file travels truly along the line, and be sure that

(Drawing #3) Types of files and ways they are positioned for executing the blade-ricasso transition.

(31) Finishing the bevel next to the ricasso.

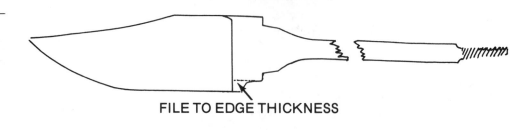

FILE TO EDGE THICKNESS

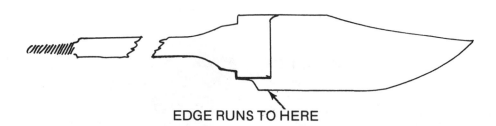

EDGE RUNS TO HERE

(32) Extending the bevel into the ricasso, using the safe-edge square file.

(33) Checking for symmetry.

the smooth or safe side is down on the blade. When the above is accomplished, you'll note a very ugly little bit of steel remains there. Drawing #4 shows the area. Now we are going to turn this into a little "trick" bit that isn't seen too often. Pick up that square tapering file with the single safe edge and place the safe edge against the line of the ricasso. Using this for a guide, file carefully so that it begins to look like photo 32. Keep at it until the edge is down as indicated in the drawing. Use the flat Swiss pattern file (with two safe edges) to dress it up all around. When it looks like photo 33, wrap the little file with some 220 grit paper and try to remove all the scratches. Be careful and do a good job. This is a highly visible point and we want it to look right.

All throughout this chapter so far, we have stressed that none of the filing on the blade should come down to the edge. There is a reason. The file is an efficient tool for removing steel. Files work well, but have one serious drawback. The teeth of the file don't stay free from particles of the material they are filing. That is why in both Section II, Chapter 1, "How To Make A Knife By The Stock Removal Method," and Section IV, Chapter 1, "Tools," the frequent use of the file card or brush is stressed. It is a necessary tool for those who use files. With constant attention, the file can be kept relatively free from these particles. But you can't *depend* on it. Just when all is going well and the cut is smooth, a single steel particle can hang up between the teeth of the file, turn up, and become a jagged tooth that rakes across the surface, gouging a deep, ugly scratch.

Such incidents are unimportant at any stage except the final smoothing and truing. But if it happens then, it is decidely unfunny. So we take no chances. We leave the files and go to abrasive paper.

This coated paper is called "wet or dry" by most auto supply stores and it's usually silicon carbide grit. We will be using grit sizes from 180 to 600. The primary "safety" factor is that you just can't get a deeper scratch from this paper than the size of the grit. It also cuts in any direction. It can be shaped to order by simply varying the support that you use. In other words, if you wrap it around a flat surface, the paper will cut flat. If the support is round, angular, or has a radius, the paper will conform to that shape and will cut and smooth in just that way. The beginner may be tempted to try to stretch out the use of the paper beyond its effective cutting life. Unfortunately, the sharp cutting ability of this paper has a short life, and if used beyond a certain point, it results in largely wasted effort. Learn quickly how much to expect, and replace the paper at once when it stops working for you.

In practice, we started the use of 180 grit size on the ricasso of

(34) Begin hand-sanding the ricasso first.

the knife(34). Being used to this way of finishing, we simply use a file about 3/4-inch wide, with fine teeth, for the support. The paper is cut so that it is about 1/4-inch wider on each side than the file. This extra width can be turned up on the edges of the file for safety: it also helps keep the paper from slipping. In the same vein, the end of the paper is turned over the end of the file and grasped with the thumb and first finger of the left hand. The other end of the paper is held by the right hand in a similar manner. The key to finishing with this abrasive paper is to cover the working area with uniform scratches (grooves left by the grit size) before moving to a smaller grit. The first use of the paper with the coarse 180 grit is to remove all of the file marks. You will find that there are some file marks which are deeper than the rest. Get all of these marks out. At this stage, the paper can be run across the work in a random pattern until the last of the file marks is gone. Then finish up with all the scratch marks going in one direction.

After the ricasso areas are cleaned up, do the same with the blade. As you work on the blade, keep your goal in mind, the concept of flatness.

After a few cuts, any low or high spots on the blade will begin to show up. This coarse grit cuts fairly fast if you keep it sharp. Use strokes that angle across the blade in both directions, again to help get to the true flat we are after. When both sides seem to be level and flat, stroke several times on each side to establish a pattern of scratches that all run in the same diagonal direction.

The tang of the blade needs some attention. The end will be threaded and the whole tang must be tapered slightly toward the threaded end. Determine the length of tang to be threaded and then clamp up that portion close to the vise jaws. Work with a flat bastard file and cut the edges of the tang equally on both sides until the part to be threaded is square. Then with the file, round off the corners until the tang becomes a round rod. Don't reduce the diameter because we will use a die made for a 3/16-inch screw.

(35) Tapering the tang toward the thread end.

(36) Threading the end of the tang.

(37) Changing from 180 grit to 220 grit shows quickly.

Before threading, place the steel support bar stock in the vise, clamp up the blade with Vise Grips (don't forget to pad the steel with leather scrap). Using the single cut flat file, taper the tang from the guard area to the end. This will greatly simplify the fitting of the guard (35).

Now clamp up the tang, apply some thread cutting oil (36), and proceed to thread that rounded tang.

Before we start the hand-sanding, consider that when this knife goes to the heat treater, all the marks, scars and scratches that go into the fire will be there when the blade comes out and many times harder! Filing that hardened steel is out of the question. Sanding before heat-treating is the only way, and the less remaining to do, the better. It is apparent that these hand methods require more careful finishing before heat-treating than do other methods. One should also make very sure of his heat-treater. The best way may be to call up a knifemaker of repute who lives in your region, and ask him for the name of his heat treater. A good treater will return your blade with nary a pit or surface defect, if that is the way you send it to him.

When we left the blade, the whole surface was sanded down flat and true with 180 grit paper. Now we switch to 220 grit and repeat the process, but change the direction of the sanding strokes. This is a valuable method because it indicates both where you are working and how much has to come off the steel surface for each grit (37).

This photo shows what the different direction of scratches does to the reflection of the light off of the blade. It is this reflected light that becomes our guide. You'll note that most of the scratch marks are at about a 45-degree angle to the length of the blade. This is a rule but not a hard and fast one. The exceptions come when sanding around the ricasso area where that transition between blade edge and ricasso occurs. In this area, the paper with the support (a file or other metal flat surface) is moved sideways, either toward or away from the ricasso, while the file itself is at a 90-degree angle to the edge. The sanding surface is moved sideways across the blade with a diagonal motion. It does leave a scratch pattern of about 45 degrees, and it takes a bit of practice. But doing it this way allows the sanding to come right to the ricasso and, with a bit of paper overlapping the edge of the support, the transitional bevel itself can also be smoothed. When that angle comes to the edge of the paper and its support, you merely lift the whole sanding device very slightly while stroking. Keep the surface level with the blade surface, and let the very edge of the paper do the work. Controlled, continuous movement is the key here, and it too requires practice.

Each succeedingly smaller grit size must be used until all the marks of the previous sanding are gone. Inspect your work very carefully as you proceed. If you miss some scratches, they **will** show up and all you can do is go back and get rid of them.

Continue this operation until you reach and use the 400 grit size. It is easier to go from 220 to 360 to 400 than to skip the 360. Now, 400 grit size is not a bad finish. You will be able to see some distinct reflections now, especially if you have kept using sharp, fresh paper.

Now let's take care of some other aspects of this knifemaking, the hard way. With our blade finished to a 400 grit surface, we must turn our attention to the back of the knife. Earlier, we scribed a line down the center and now we are going to file a ridge here, using that line to keep us centered. All that is needed is a slight dropping of the handle of a file to achieve this small double bevel (38). Using plenty of padding (leather works fine), clamp up the blade and file toward the center, using a rather fine flat file and angling away at about 45 degrees. The actual back bevel angle can be slight, because its

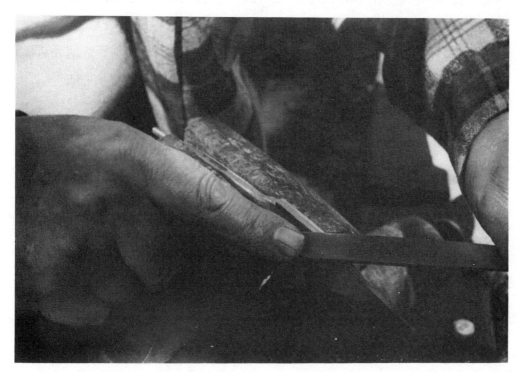

(38) Filing the angle on the back of the blade.

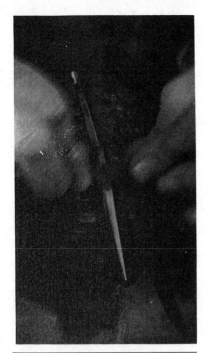

(39) Finishing the back with paper abrasive.

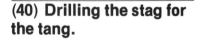

(40) Drilling the stag for the tang.

purpose is purely decorative. It takes only a little filing to cause the light to reflect and to break up an otherwise rather boring line. When the back of the knife has been filed to the center, continue by using the paper abrasive(39), going from coarse to fine just as on the blade. Keep a sharp eye on the centerline, for it must stay true to look right.

When making knives by other methods, if the ricasso shoulders are slightly off, they can still be altered after heat treatment by the careful use of a bench grinder. But our hand-tooled blade will come back just slightly softer than a good file, and there will be no way we can correct any problem. So we are going to fit the guard before heat treatment. By the way, this is a practice used in the Loveless shop with very good results.

Also you'll recall that while our design called for a curved tang, we sawed it straight. As we have already chosen the handle material, we are going to fit that now too, handle against guard and guard against shoulders. This should guarantee that all will go together properly.

It is a small matter to prepare the handle material. The piece of stag is first sawed to length and close to the final size.

We have our sketch of the knife, and from that we are able to determine where we want the hole in the butt end of the stag to come out. Considering the curve of the tang and the angle that the butt is sawed, the threaded portion should come out at 90 degrees to the butt.

It is essential to be careful with alignment when drilling the hole through the stag. Using a brace and a twist type drill, we center the drill in the small end of the stag and drill toward the center of the stag (if that hole were continued, it would come out near the top of the butt). We drill about halfway through(40). Then we reverse the stag and drill again toward the center. We are able to feel when the two holes join.

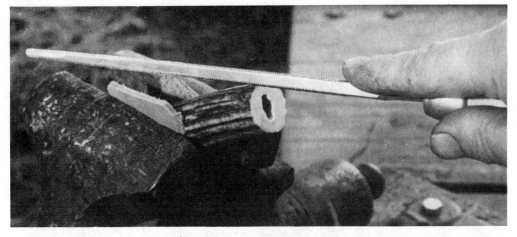

(41)The rasp used to make the tang fit.

We have what is called a "rat-tailed" round file or rasp. Hopefully, you have kept on good terms with the man with the grinder for we wish to grind opposite sides flat, leaving a thickness of a bit over 3/16-inch(41). With this tool, we can rasp out the interior of the tang hole until there is enough room for the curved tang to go through the stag. We also use the same tool to shape the front of the stag to accommodate the larger part of the tang.

(42)Polishing the guard face on 600 grit wet-or-dry.

With the stag at this point, we'll start on the guard. Making the guard is also discussed in Section II, Chapter I, "How To Make A Knife By The Stock Removal Method." The way that we make the guard can vary somewhat. We prepare the brass by finishing the surface with up to 600 grit paper, going through the grits as described earlier, to remove all but the finest scratches(42). Then we bring up the polish with a cloth-backed polishing material called crocus cloth, a material consisting of a coating of red ferric oxide on a stiff backing. It's the same size sheet as the wet-or-dry paper we've been using.

This finish is very close to the mirror polish obtained by machine buffing.

(43)Drilling the guard. Primitive knifemaking!

(44)Opening up the tang slot with the file.

(45)Finishing for the best possible fit.

We scribe a centerline, mark off the width of the tang, and center-punch for the first hole. It always pays to make the hole smaller than the final size; this is another ''safe'' procedure in beginning knifemaking. So we drill(43) a line of holes that are CLOSE to each other, and then cut out the webbing between with a small round file used in sharpening chain saws (44). It's fast, and as long as you control the file, it does a fine job.

From then on making the guard is much as described in Section II, Chapter I. The photo (45) shows how the line-up of file and reflection keeps the file cutting perfectly straight, and photo (46)

(46)Note how this file has been altered for this job.

(47)The visual result of a careful job.

shows how the small flat bastard file has been ground for this particular job. It becomes apparent now why the tang was tapered. Fitting the guard very close requires that almost each stroke of the file allows the guard to move slightly toward the shoulders. It is so easy to take too much off that you must try the guard for fit often. The hole in the guard must match the taper just before the shoulders of the blade. This must be done with great care, keeping the file straight and true. This is time consuming but well worth the effort. There is great satisfaction in having a fit that shows only a hair line where blade and guard join (47).

If the fitting of the guard was near perfect, it went into place with a hard push and stayed there; if not, perhaps you'll choose to solder it by one of the methods described in Section II, Chapter I. Just one word about soldering that can never be repeated too often: get everything CLEAN beforehand. Clean is at least half the battle of a good soldering joint.

Now it's time to get the stag into a perfect fit against the guard. This photo shows the tang being slightly bent by anchoring the tang end in the vise and applying pressure with the hands(48). Try to bend it gently but firmly. The tang is still soft and moves easily. As soon as the tang will slip through the stag, check where the threaded

(48)Bending the tang to the curve of the stag block.

(49) The tang must center the hole—keep working.

(50) Now it looks right.

(51) Remember the guard—give yourself room here.

end lays (50). This photo shows the tang end coming out too close to the bottom of the hole. Keep at it until it is centered (51). Now turn your attention to the fit of the stag to the tapered part of the tang. You may have to remove the guard to true this perfectly (52). Be sure that the stag goes forward just a little past where the back of the guard will eventually be. This allows room to fit the stag to the flat of the guard.

With the guard back in place, try the stag on for fit. See if one part touches first, when looking at it from the side. Then look from the top and see if the end of the stag is square with the back of the guard. If material must be removed from the stag, one way is to clamp up that big, smooth file in the vise: hold the stag firmly in

both hands, and slowly and steadily draw it against the teeth. With a little practice to get the feel, you can get a very true surface this way.

When this joint is perfect, it is then time to pay attention to the butt end of the stag. Because of the pithy nature of the stag, we will use a butt cap and a round ''nut'' that will hold the whole thing together. This butt cap should be made of the same 1/4-inch brass as the guard, so cut out a square big enough to cover the whole surface of the knife handle end. Center this square of brass and drill a 3/16-inch hole right through so that the cap will slip over the threaded tang. The ''nut'' came to us via A.G. Russell and Company, and is a piece of round brass stock with a threaded hole. It is used in the Morseth knife, but you'd better look for a plain brass nut instead, which will work just as well. (The correct use of this round ''nut'' is shown in Drawing #1(2).)

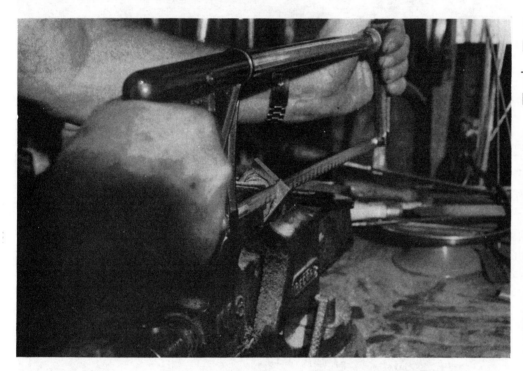

(52)Cutting the rough butt cap.

(53)File right to the lay-out line.

When the brass is slipped over the tang, hold it steady and use a marking pen to trace the rough outline. Remove the brass and saw it roughly to that outline (52). Then clamp up close in a vise and file it to shape.

In any case, file it to the line(53). It is now necessary to fit the butt end of the stag to the butt cap. True this end the same way until the butt cap fits without any gaps. Now this just isn't as easy to do as it is to write about. It will take time to learn how to get that perfectly flat surface to mate with the brass. It is the mark of good work to have all those joints without visible flaws.

Everything that we can do to the soft blade has been done, and it's time to send the blade to the heat treater. Tell him that you want a finish hardness of 58 to 59 RC and that you want no surface change. The blade will be returned slightly grey and ready for finishing. Go over all the surfaces with 400 grit paper again and make everything bright.

The following is optional, but it was the way this blade was handled. A propane torch was fired up, and with the blade and ricasso wrapped in very damp cloth, the tang was heated back from the end about 3 inches. When the color was a light blue (soft) we took away the flame and, keeping the wet cloth on the blade, allowed it to cool. We feel that this is just a bit of a safety measure. The threaded portion of the tang is now quite soft and will resist any inclination to break if the knife is dropped butt first onto some rock or hard floor.

(54)A coffee-can lid makes a good epoxy dish.

(55)Coat the guard and tang with plenty of epoxy.

Everything has been prepared for handle assembly so, if and when the handle seems to be fitting well, it is time to get out the epoxy and put it all together. Here, the epoxy is mixed in the lids from various grocery store containers (54). A soldering brush is used to give a thorough coat to all the surfaces (55). Even though the tang hole will be filled with epoxy, it seems the safest way to make sure all the metal is coated. It is important with steels such as 0-1, for they rust very quickly and if moisture gets into the tang area, it will surely corrode any exposed surface. The epoxy is thick and makes it possible to get some into the hole and then sort of rotate the stag until it has coated all the surfaces. Then we let it slide toward the back end, and while it is there we put it over the tang and bring it down against the guard. This way, there won't be a lot of messy epoxy pushing out the top and bottom. With the handle in place, the void at the top is filled with epoxy, the butt coated with a thin layer, and the brass is similarly coated and put into place. The nut is started, and then run up tight(56). Right then, clean off all the extra epoxy with a damp cloth.

When all is done, the knife looks like the one in photo 57 with the guard and butt cap still in the raw state. Now set the completed assembly aside until the epoxy has set up hard. Now is a good time to take a break from your work. Go fishing, and give the epoxy a full 24 hours to set up.

(56)The end of the assembly job—run the nut down tight.

(57)Now go fishing for a day or so.

(58)Protect that blade!!

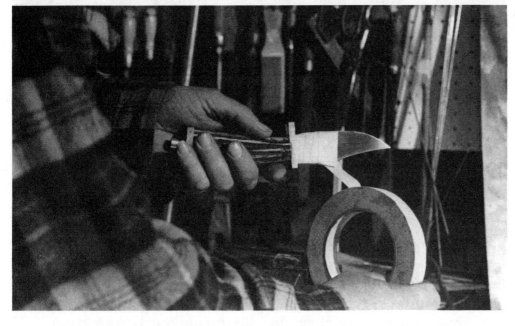

With the epoxy hard, wrap the blade with masking tape (58). It is just too easy to mar the blade, and the tape is pretty cheap insurance.

(59)Finish shaping the butt cap.

(60)Work closely and carefully.

(61)Cut the stag down to the guard.

(62)Clean up the butt cap nut.

From now on, every time we clamp up the knife in the vise, we use scrap leather for protection. It also helps hold the handle, which is an irregular shape, very firmly.

The rough shaping is done now on the brass (59). The butt cap is brought to size. The roughest work is done with the handle clamped up. The finish filing is done on a piece of leather that is laid over the partially open vise jaws (60).

Next, the stag is brought down to the level of the guard on both sides (61).

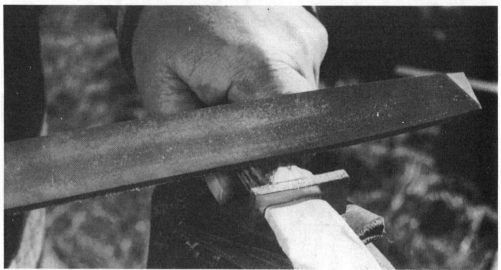

We finish up the butt cap first, by filing a bevel around it (62). While this is still in the rough stage, we have cut into the bottom of the stag just forward of the butt and filed off some of the top. We are using a medium-sized half round file with a crossing tooth pattern and it requires frequent cleaning with the file brush to keep it cutting right. After filing, the stag is smoothed up with strips of a cloth-backed roll abrasive(63), as described fully in Section II, Chapter 1.

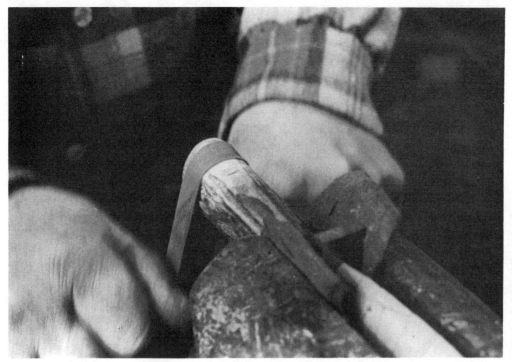

Now we turn to the guard. The first action is to wrap the stag above the guard to protect it. The curve of the guard (64) is done before shaping the rest of it. This provides us with more working

(65) Shaping the sides of the guard.

surface and makes it somewhat easier to judge our work. After that, the guard itself is filed to shape, top and bottom (65). We have decided on a small thumb rest on the top of the guard. This filing is done with a straight round file. Then all the brass is smoothed with strips of the roll abrasive torn into the appropriate widths (66). Next the whole area is smoothed with either this roll abrasive or sheets of abrasive paper wrapped over the appropriate backing.

(66) Fine-sanding the top of the guard.

(67)Finishing the butt.

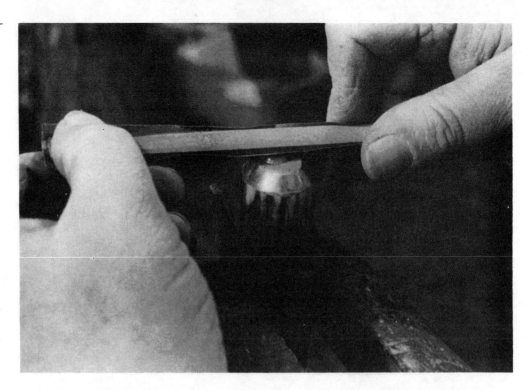

On inspection, the butt cap seems to fit the knife and so we finish it with paper wrapped over a flat fine-toothed file (67).

The whole handle is brought to a smooth 600 grit finish, except for the stag; we leave its natural texture alone.

It must be emphasized that all of the brass and the stag that has been shaped must be absolutely free from scratches if the high luster finish is to look right.

The back side of a used abrasive strip is charged with polishing compound, and that side is applied to the surface to be polished with a "shoeshine" motion. It works on metal or stag.

Now is also the time to introduce the polishing stick, a piece of wood, long, narrow and flat, that has had either felt or leather glued to one surface. It too, is charged with polishing compound and used in a fast filing kind of motion. It is good for flat areas.

It is a matter of personal preference whether the blade is finished before the handle is put on or after. It is somewhat easier to hold the blade before but it is safer to wait until the very last moment.

A hand-rubbed finish means a 500 or 600 grit finish, with all the tiny scratch marks running the length of the blade.

The finish achieved with 400 grit paper is just beginning to show reflections. When we move to 600, the paper is wrapped around a brass bar; 1/4-inch by 1-inch by 8-inches is fine. The lower edges are slightly rounded on this bar so that there is no danger of a sharp edge pressing the paper down and making a distinctly different scratch pattern.

The 600 grit loads up very quickly and must be changed often. This is such a fine grit that it doesn't seem to matter how you use it to remove the 400 grit scratches. It will take very close examination to be sure that all of the coarser grit marks are gone. When you are satisfied, change from the brass support to the little device shown (Drawing #5). Cut little rectangles of the 600 grit paper just wide enough to cover the bottom of the rubber and long enough to

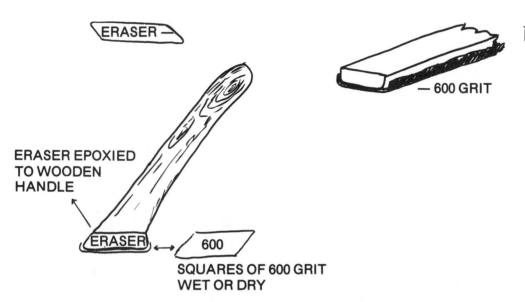

ERASER

— 600 GRIT

ERASER EPOXIED TO WOODEN HANDLE

ERASER

600

SQUARES OF 600 GRIT WET OR DRY

lap up over the ends. By using this "push" stick, a great deal of pressure can be brought to bear on the steel. Now, all the motions should be along the line of the blade. The more the lines run the same direction, the more reflection you will see.

When the blade itself looks fairly uniform but with some **uneven** areas, use only new 600 grit squares of paper and start at the junction of ricasso and edge. Using a lot of pressure, draw SLOWLY toward the point. Do this only once with each piece of paper. The object is to obtain a perfectly uniform surface. Try until it looks good, and then STOP!

If you are doing this with the handle on the knife, you must wrap the handle with enough leather scraps so that when the vise jaws are tightened, there is no movement.

(68) The completed knife. Whew!!

Finally, your knife should look something like this (68). Has it all been worth it? Only you can answer.

SECTION III
ALTERNATE METHODS

FLAT GRINDING

Michael Collins is an artist known for his flat ground knives with marvelous multicolored scrimshawed ivory handles. Less widely known is his intense interest in creatures of the wild and the drawings in color that he creates. But here we are concerned with his flat grinding techniques.

This tall, curly-headed Southern gentleman starts his blade with the same bar stock that most makers get when the steel reaches the shop. His choice is 440C and he does his own heat-treating.

---

(1) Flatten and true the blade.

---

(2) Back to the belt grinder.

Like most makers he also scribes the pattern on the stock, and cuts it to length. In his case, he removes the bigger pieces of excess metal with an abrasive cut-off wheel. The profile is trued and smoothed up on the contact wheel of a **Square Wheel Grinder**. The blade blank is then flattened and trued on a 6-inch horizontal belt grinder. Most bar stock looks fairly flat and straight (1), but in truth it has some dips and pits that must be removed at this stage if trouble is to be avoided down the line. He waits until the blade is profiled simply because there is less steel to grind flat and true.

From the wide belt grinder, the blade is returned to the grinder, now used with the platen attachment in place (2). He uses a 60 grit belt with this set-up to remove metal quickly. He stays clear of critical areas, concentrating on getting rid of bulk (3).

From here on, the wide belt grinder, with a 60 grit belt to start, is the machine used to finish grinding the blade. This grinder turns toward the operator and runs somewhat slower than normal to gain more power from the 1-horsepower electric motor. The right-hand side of the platen has been filed to a nice round, smooth radius and all the grinding is done from that side. Note

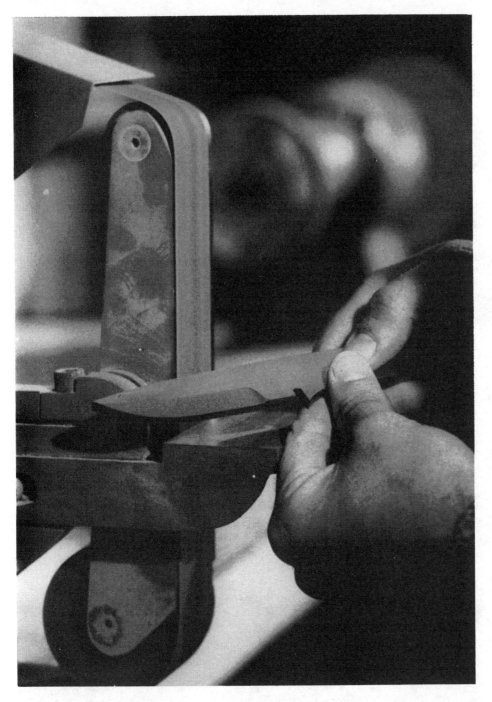

(3) First, work to reduce bulk.

(4) Use the push stick.

(5) Notice that the point is still nearly full thickness.

(6) The thickness permits proper use of the push stick.

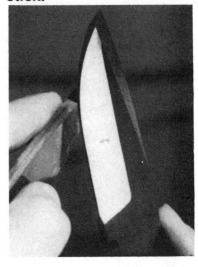

the push stick (4). Also note that the knife point is left nearly full thickness (5). The reason is that this blade design has a false edge and the thickness at the end gives a surface and edge for the push stick to push against (6).

At the same time as this rough grinding is being done, the radius between blade and ricasso is trued and equalled.

At this stage, the edge is established either true to a scribed centerline or true to the accurate sense of ''feel'' that has come to Michael after grinding hundreds of blades.

Michael runs the belt over the working edge of the platen so that about 1/4-inch is unsupported. Depending on how much more or less is overhung, the radius from ricasso to blade is either abrupt or gradual.

Now, attention is turned to the point (7). The tang is raised and the point is ground equally on each side. At first no attempt is made to blend the grinding on the point with that of the blade proper. There is a noticeable difference where the two grinds come together.

(7) With the tang raised, the point is ground.

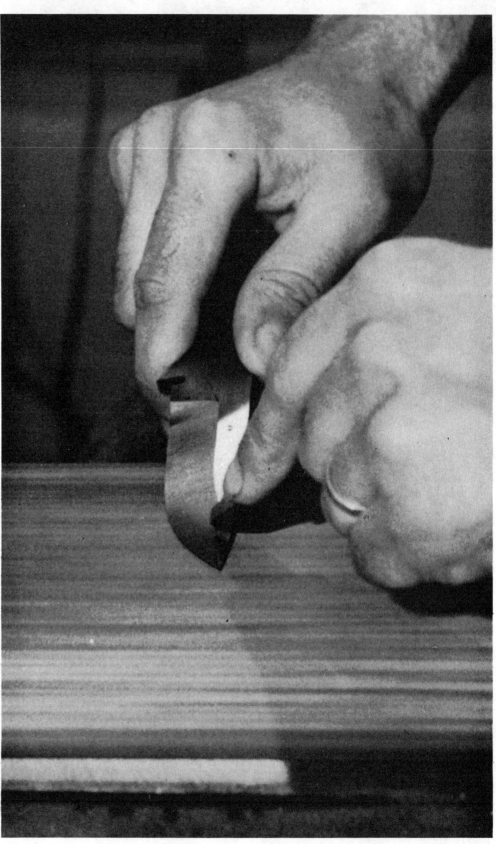

There is meat still left on the blade — enough to do any truing or balancing to blade, ricasso radius, or point. Now a new 120 grit belt is put on and Michael brings it all into balance and smooth lines. He works the blade to very near the final size. At first with the finer belt, he uses the push stick, but near the finish of the grind only his fingers are used(8). With the 220 belt, the angle of grind is changed and with the scratches running on this new angle it is easy to see any of the old 60 grit marks and remove them. When all the grind lines run the same way, and the blade passes a critical examination(9), it is ready for finishing.

(8) Nearing completion, the blade is hand-held.

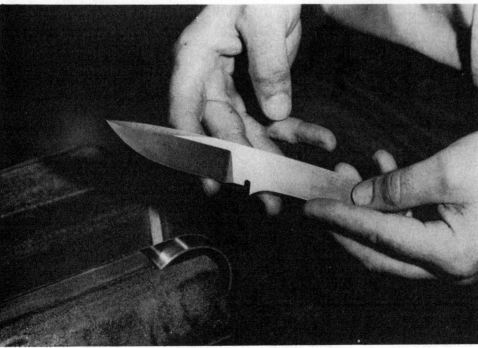

(9) The blade is now ready to finish.

**SOLDERING
THE GUARD**

Corbet Sigman solders hidden tang guards somewhat differently. The guard is partially finished first(1). The face of the guard is polished and both blade and guard are completely cleaned. Let's repeat that, CLEANED. The guard is pressed into position on the blade and then the blade is placed face down in a vise. (Protect the blade finish with a fold of leather scrap.) Taking an automatic center punch, he drives little points or dents in the back of the guard against the blade. Moving these little dents of guard material against the blade serves to hold the guard in place while soldering and also forms a sort of dam against the free flow of solder. Remember, the tighter the fit the better the solder job, both in neatness and strength. The blade is left point down in the vise and flux is carefully applied around the joint. Many fluxes change characteristics just about when ''flow'' temperature is reached. By watching carefully it is possible to know just about when to apply solder successfully. Corbett uses a flux called **Alpha Steel Grip #90** made by Alpha Laboratories. It is designed especially for stainless steel but works well with other metals. Corbet feels that there are many solders that will work well. All would be silver bearing with a melting point around 420 degrees F.

Now the guard and tang are heated up with a propane torch (2) and when the correct temperature is reached he applies a ''blob'' of solder at each end of the tang-guard joint. The blade is turned over in the vise and the torch is applied to the top of the guard (not the blade). A combination of capillary action, metal affinity and wetting causes the blobs of solder, now under the guard, to melt and flow upward. A small pointed iron drawn along the joint helps the solder run around the joint (3). If done correctly, a fine fillet of solder circles the blade and guard.

(1) Partially finish the guard.

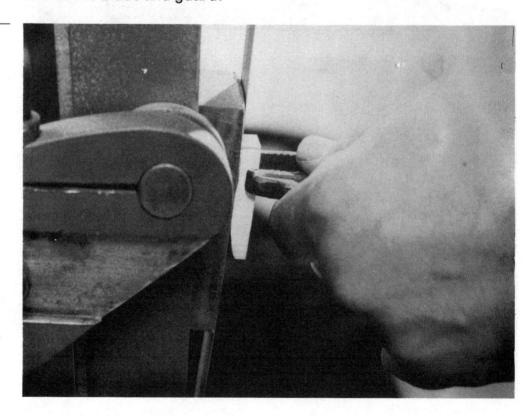

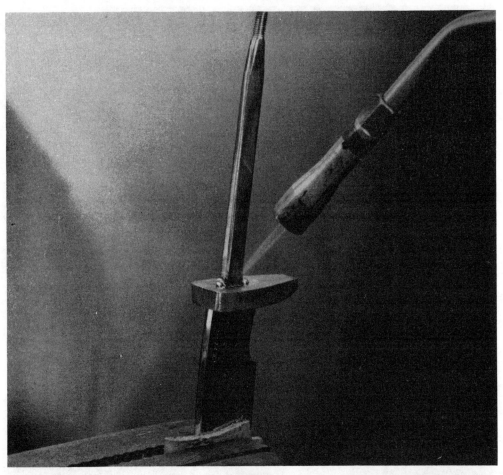

(2) Heat the guard and tang and apply solder.

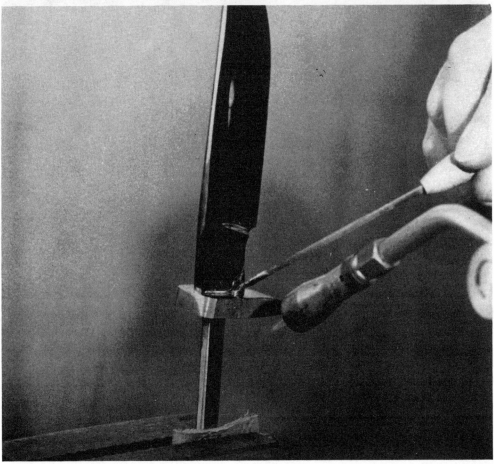

(3) Draw small pointed iron along joint.

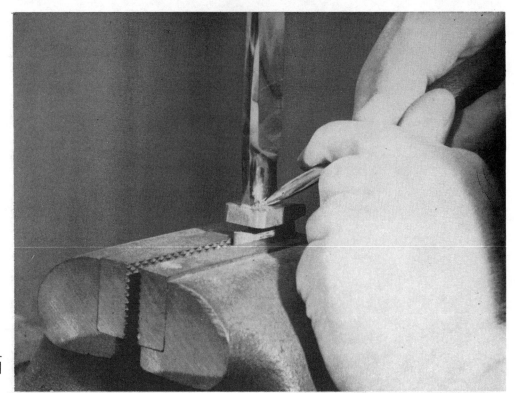

(4) Burnish solder around joint.

(5) Remove excess solder and polish joint.

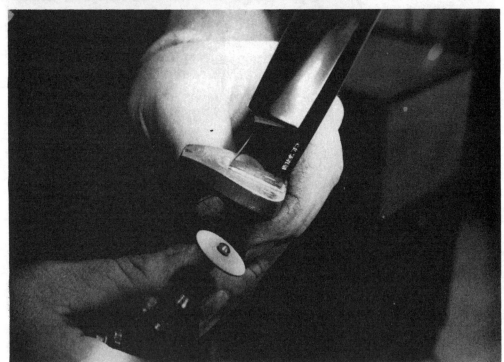

At times it will be necessary to apply a touch of solder. Any excess can be quickly wiped off with a rag. When the solder has set, Corbet pushes a polished steel burnisher around the joint(4). This forms the fillet uniformly and seals any porosity that may be present.

You'll note in the next picture (5) that Corbet uses a **MOTO** tool and a fine rubber polishing wheel dressed to an edge (designated **WR888** and available from Paul H. Gesswen and Co., 235 Park Avenue South, New York, New York 10003). With this tool he removes any excess solder and polishes the joint itself.

The juncture between the knife guard and the blade is one of the most visible indicators of craftsmanship. For the amateur, a neat fit is a matter of pride; for the professional, it is expected in today's quality knife market. A few well-known makers are able to achieve a fit that is almost undetectable at the blade-guard joint. The technique developed mainly in Utah and most of the Utah makers employ it. The description of this technique comes directly from the shop of Buster Warenski, located in Richfield, Utah.

The blade shown in this section is a bootleg dagger about 5 inches long, and the guard will be double. This kind of construction calls for the guard to be slipped over the tang, coming to rest against the shoulders of the blade as previously prepared.

We're starting with a piece of nickel silver 1/4-inch x 3/4-inch x 1-1/2 inches cut from bar stock. The first step is of prime importance, as you will see later. Although the guard stock comes with an even, smooth finish, we want a mirror finish on both flats. Shown here (1) is a standard piece of wet-dry abrasive paper that has been taped to a smooth, flat surface. The flats are leveled and refined through successive grit sizes to either 400 or 500 grit size. When all the scratches are eliminated except the finest, the edges of the stock are gripped by hand or Vise Grips and polished on the high-speed buffer until each side is mirror finished. It is a good idea to have one particular buff, 6- or 8-inch sewn cotton, just for use with nickel silver and brass.

(1) Level and refine guard material prior to mirror finishing.

Place the polished guard stock on a flat surface and lay the blade over it as shown (2). Center and lightly scribe a line along the edges of the tang to the shoulders. These lines will be the extreme ends of the tang slot. Next, lightly scribe a centerline the length of the guard material. You will use this line for center punching. Select a drill size 1/16-inch under the size of the maximum tang thickness. Carefully space a series of center-punch marks down the centerline so that when the holes are drilled each hole nearly touches its neighbor. Use caution so that no hole edge extends past the scribed lines that mark the slot ends. After drilling the holes, Buster uses a short drill to remove the web left between the holes. The illustration (3) shows a slightly rough rectangular hole with plenty of stock left to file-fit to the tang. As a matter of interest, pictured here is a carbide router bit designed for slow, fine metal removal (4). This picture was taken in the shop of Corbet Sigman. He uses this router bit to clean up the hole after drilling and although somewhat slower, it leaves a neater, cleaner hole.

(2) Lay blade on guard material for marking widest part of tang.

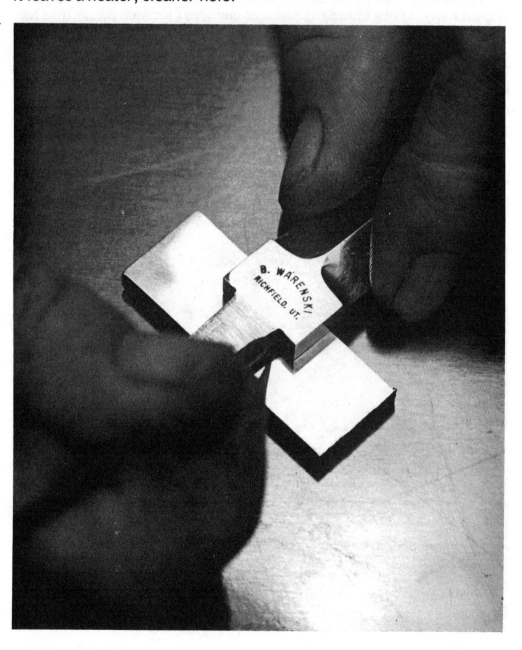

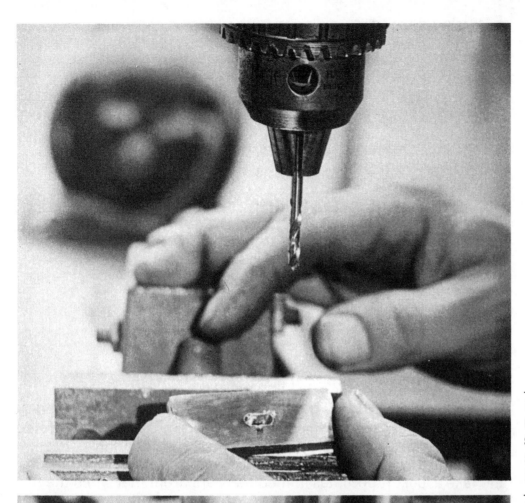

(3) Drill a slightly rough rectangular hole, being sure to leave plenty of stock to file-fit to the tang.

(4) Use carbide router bit to clean up hole.

Note in the photographs how a drill press vise is attached to a compound vise. They are very good friends to have around a small knife shop and are almost indispensable in many ways.

(5) File with ground ("safe") side.

This ordinary file is a thin, flat bastard with one edge ground away and narrow enough to enter the guard slot (5). The ground side becomes "safe" and is very useful in this and other filing operations. Now clamp the guard edges in a vise, insert the file (6) and take a look. It becomes immediately apparent that when the file in your hand and the one reflected from the mirror finished guard surface are in line, the file is cutting at exactly 90 degrees to the polished flat surface of the guard stock. With a little practice and care, the guard slot can be filed **very accurately**.

(6) Filing guard.

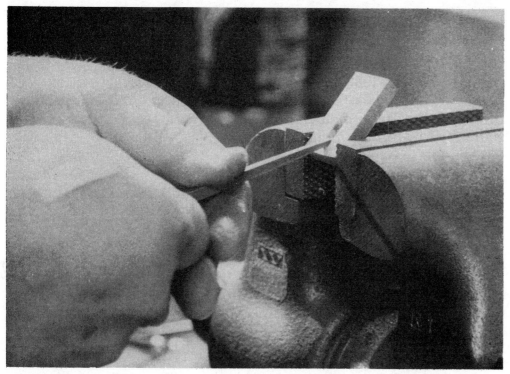

(7) File tang hole to fit shoulder of blade.

Now it is simply a matter of filing the guard to fit (using the "safe" side of the file to work on only one surface at a time). If the blade tang has only a slight taper from end to guard area, care should be taken once the guard is filed enough to fit over the end of the tang. Try the tang many times while filing. Toward the end of the process only a bit of filing can make a great deal of difference. Of course, the inner ends of the tang hole will have to be filed to fit the shoulder of the blade(7). The last fit should be a hard hand-press to position. If done properly, this fit should be a matter of some pride(8).

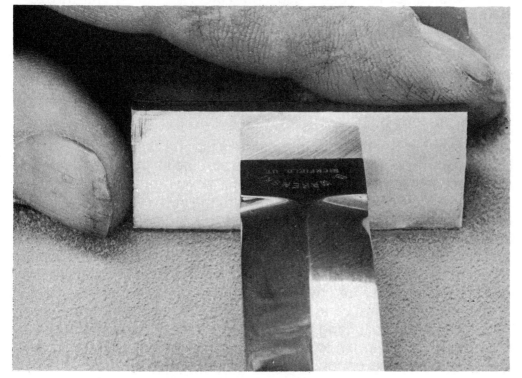

(8) Solderless guard finished. Note the hairline fit.

The hidden tang method of handle construction is one of the oldest and most commonly used in the making of knives, swords and many other hand tools. When forging was the universal way of forming blades, a narrow tang was simply drawn out from the body of the blade. Today's stock removal methods call for tang forming either by sawing or grinding.

Drawing # 1.

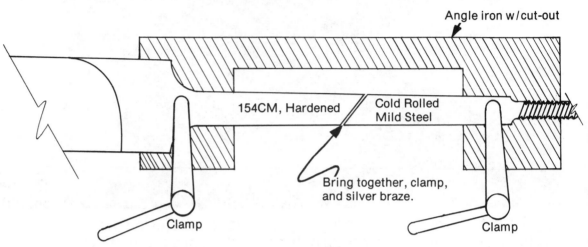

Angle iron w/cut-out

154CM, Hardened

Cold Rolled Mild Steel

Bring together, clamp, and silver braze.

Clamp

Clamp

(1) The area just behind the guard is most important.

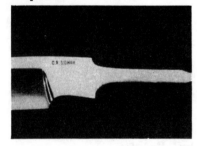

Because modern high-speed tool steel is nearly impossible to selectively "draw down" to a relatively soft or tough condition, many modern makers silver braze (silver solder or hard solder) or electric weld a piece of tough, mild (low carbon) steel onto a stubby blade tang (drawing #1). Although this way does save a bit of expensive steel, the primary purpose is to provide a tang end of soft, tough steel. It is easy to thread and allows some bending to help align the threaded end to the butt cap and handle material. Instead of mild bar steel, other makers use a mild steel rod called "all-thread" that is pre-threaded. When attached to the stubby blade tang, the sides are ground to the same thickness leaving edges with threads that will work with a nut or threaded butt.

Some prejudice exists today against the narrow or hidden tang. Narrow tang knives made by such makers as Ted Dowell and Corbet Sigman are more than adequately strong and are perfectly acceptable.

Mechanically, the area immediately behind the guard is most critical. At this point, the tang must be as wide as possible and the strongest construction demands a rather large radius or "flare" (1) from the widest dimension of the tang to the narrowest. Never grind or file abrupt shoulders for the guard as this can create dangerous stress risers. Likewise, the edges of the radius near the guard should be finely finished and without deep scratches for the same reasons. Remember that the guard for hidden tang knives is slipped over the end of the tang and fitted by filing. Grind or file a slight taper from butt end to guard area and the guard can then be fitted more easily.

A close handle to tang fit in the guard area insures maximum strength. With attention to design and construction, the hidden tang knife will be strong enough for any cutting job.

At one time a major problem that cursed knifemakers was rust. Not on the exposed blade; that could be seen and corrected. But it was hidden rust on the tang, resulting from moisture that crept in through the joints, that was the headache. Narrow tangs could be sealed somewhat better than full tang knives, but not by much. Two modern products, if they are used, make that problem almost nonexistent. They are epoxy and high quality stain-resistant steel.

Epoxy, of course, does more than seal out moisture. It also bonds handle material to steel far better than anything else has before.

Jim Small uses a type of epoxy in a way that may be unique in full tang handle construction. He has taken advantage of a kind of epoxy called quick-set or "five minute."

(Author's note: A slow-setting epoxy is recommended for beginning knifemakers.)

To go back a bit, we'll start at the point where the tang has been tapered and the guard fixed. Jim uses the knife tang for a pattern(1) and pencils a line on the handle material(2). He does the same on the fiber line. He then bandsaws the handle material to the line, and cuts the liner with stout shears(3).

APPLYING SCALE HANDLES

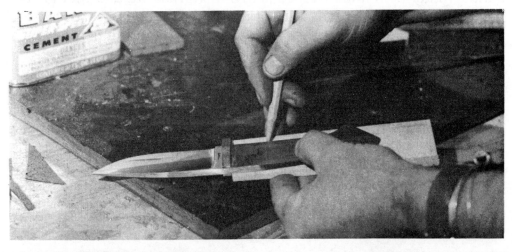

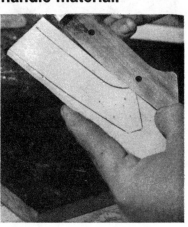

(1) Using a tang makes a good pattern.

(2) A pencil outline on the handle material.

(3) Cutting the liner.

Now is a good time to say that this is an easy and fast way to apply slabs or scales to a full tang knife ONLY if everything is flat and it fits as it should.

(4) Scoring the fiber.

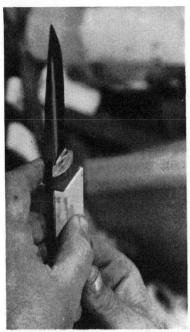

(5)Test for fit before proceeding.

The tapered tang has already been checked for flatness; the handle material in this instance is 3/8-inch Micarta, and that is very flat as the maker receives it. Note that the fiber is scored with a file(4), and is bent 90 degrees, and that it fits both the tang and the guard.

Everything is tried for fit (5) and the Micarta slabs are slightly roughened on flat sheet 220 abrasive paper, on a flat surface. The tang is also cleaned thoroughly.

The various parts are laid out so they are ready. The left side slab and liner are placed so that the correct surface is ready for the tang in the sequence that they'll be applied.

(6)Mix the epoxy and remember, it sets up in 5 minutes.

The epoxy is now mixed, and remember, it sets up in five minutes (6). Quickly, one side of the tang is coated (7) and the fiber liner is slid into position. (This ''sliding'' is deliberate. It

(7)Work fast, proceed with one side at a time.

138

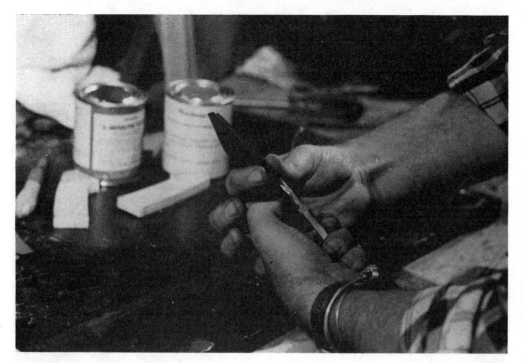

(8)"Slide" and press on the liner.

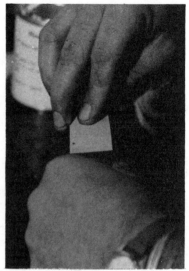

(9)Apply the slab.

minimizes the formation of air pockets.) The liner is pressed firmly onto the tang (8) and the outer surface is swiftly coated with epoxy. The coat of epoxy is thick enough to allow the slab to be slid into position(9). After a quick check to be sure that the fit is right, the knife and slab are held in position for a very brief time. In a matter of a very few minutes the slab is firmly in place. Of course, only enough epoxy is mixed at one time to do one handle slab.

(10)Drill the tang hole.

(11)Now, both handles are drilled through.

Now that the epoxy is set, the excess is cleaned off and the knife is taken to the drill press. The correct drill is selected and a hole is drilled through the tang hole and the slab(10). Both holes are done and the knife is returned to the bench, and the other handle is applied the same way as the first. Then again to the drill press, where the drill is run through the existing holes and through the second slab(11).

Now a counterbore is chucked up and the holes are all counterbored to receive the escutcheon bolts (12). The quill travel is limited so that these counterbored holes are drilled to a predetermined depth.

(12) Counterbore the holes.

(13)Fill the handle holes.

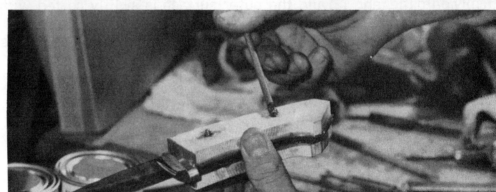

(14)Tighten the handle bolts.

The holes are filled with epoxy (13) and the bolts tightened (14). The knife, with the slabs in place, is now ready for the handle shaping.

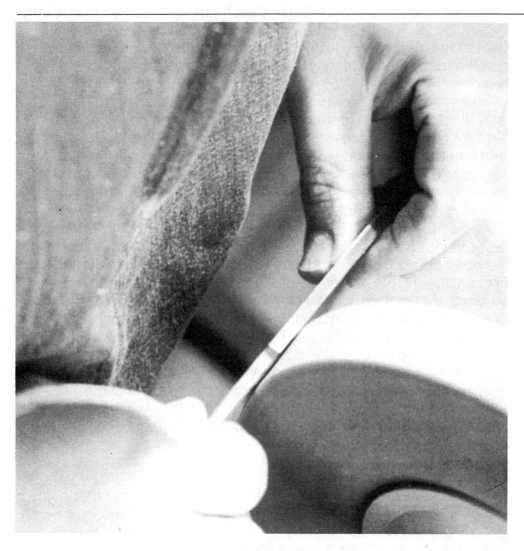

(1) Alternate finishing with compound bevels.

At a knife show, one of the first things that the pilgrim asks on seeing tables loaded with gleaming steel blades is, ''How do you ever **do** that?'' Privately, the average knifemaker may be silently asking the same question. In today's knife world, a nearly perfect blade finish is expected from all of the top makers.

Can it only be ten years ago that the big name knife came from Florida with a dull belt finish and indifferent bevels? Perhaps ''light years'' would better express what has happened in this knifemaking explosion or, if you prefer, renaissance.

Along about '69 or '70 a wonderful old bear of a man came out of Utah and hit the national scene with blades that were better ground and better polished than anything around. Harv Draper set some instant standards that are even good today. Writing in **Gun Digest,** Ken Warner said in 1971, ''Draper knives are the best finished available. It is doubtless possible to bring steel and nickel silver to a brighter, smoother and cleaner finish, but it would be very difficult indeed.''

Lacking any known technique to go by, Harvey simply learned to do a better job with a belt grinder than had been done before. He ended up with a 400 grit belt, then a worn-out 400 grit, then a 400 belt that was nude and loaded it with green chrome and belted some more. As a last step before the buffer, he turned the belt inside out, loaded the back with green chrome and kept on belting. After a spell at the high speed buffer with a cotton buff (again loaded with green chrome) those blades looked like concave mirrors, or so it seemed.

The renaissance continued and characteristically another man picked up where Harvey stopped and carried polishing to an even higher level. Corbet Sigman has the kindest heart, the purest soul and the biggest body in knifemaking. As do some of the great names in the business, Corbet **shares** his knowledge. We asked him to describe his blade polishing. The following letter, printed in its entirety, is his eloquent response:

"My primary steel is **Crucible** 154CM so this method is designed for that steel, but it is adaptable to other steels. The method outlined is intended as a guide and should not be taken as a firm unchangeable procedure. I am always searching for the new products that may change my methods. Most of the new or different things do not work, but occasionally I hit pay dirt. My only criterion for a new product is that it must do a better job. If it saves time, that is an added bonus, but I will adopt it even if it is slower in order to improve quality. One of the things that makes this profession interesting is the continual search for new products and methods. I will give you brand names for those products that I consider to be essential to my method and tell you where they may be obtained as I go through the procedure.

Step 1 — Rough Grind

"I rough grind on a 60 grit belt so we will start from that point and go through to a mirror finish. I go directly from the 60 grit belt to a 400 grit **Vitex** belt available from Garfield Industries, Midwest Buff Division, 1641 Coit Avenue, Cleveland, Ohio 44112. This is a tremendous leap from a grinding to a polishing belt, but with 154CM and the Vitex product there is no problem. I have been doing it this way for quite a long time. Scratches in some steels have a tendency to 'wipe out' and be camouflaged, so an intermediate step should be added using a 220 grit belt. It is important in grinding a blade with compound bevels to keep the belt running against the bevel with the blade in the edge up position. The same is true in polishing because the fine grit belts can destroy sharp bevel lines quickly. The area near the blade edge may be polished with the blade in the edge down position, but care should be used to prevent the belt from riding up the blade and washing over the bevels. It is absolutely necessary to remove the previous scratch pattern at each step in the polishing sequence. Polish at a different angle from the previous step and the scratch pattern is easily visible and readily removed. I should mention that there are two methods of finishing a knife with compound bevels. The alternate method is to completely mirror finish the flat areas before grinding and mirror finishing the hollow grind(1). This is probably the better method for the beginner because there is less chance of rolling (dulling) the nice sharp bevel lines. I prefer to finish the entire blade as I go because this avoids going through the sequence twice on one blade.

142

"Now to a 3450 rpm buffer (2) turning a 6x1 medium felt wheel with **Polish-O-Ray** loaded on the wheel edges. Polish-O-Ray is available from Brownell's Inc., Route 2, Box 1, Montezuma, Iowa 50171. I have tried several greaseless compounds and all of them work, but I like the one mentioned best. I polish and true up the area where the hollow grind begins in this step. The 3450 rpm buffer is used exclusively for blade finishing.

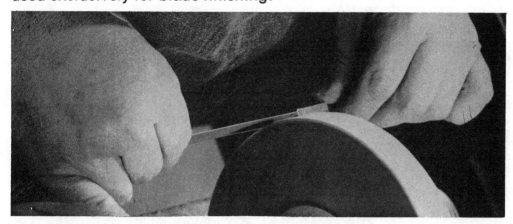

(2) A 3450 rpm buffer turning a 6x1 medium felt wheel.

Step 3 — Grind

"Back again to a used (but not worn-out) 400 grit belt loaded with bobbing compound. This compound is much used in the jewelry trade and is available from jewelers' supply houses. Mine came from Bartlett & Co., Inc., 5 South Wabash Ave., Chicago, Illinois 60603. I do not use 500 grit belts because too often I have had them cut deep scratches that required going back to a new 400 grit belt for removal. I am convinced that I have had 500 grit that were contaminated with coarser grit by the manufacturer. I have experimented with them under controlled conditions and still have had the problem of occasional deep scratches — not every belt, but enough of them to cause me to abandon 500 belts in despair. The bobbing compound-loaded 400 belt makes a very shallow pattern which can be readily removed in the next step.

NOTE:
"If grinding and polishing are done on the same grinder, it is imperative to thoroughly clean the machine before doing this step. A good blow out with compressed air is best."

Step 4 — Buff

"Back to the buffer and an 8x1 loose muslin buff loaded with 500 greaseless compound. The blade is polished lengthwise in this step (3) except where there is a danger of washing away a sharp bevel edge. The blade is held in such a manner that the buff is always sharpening the bevels instead of washing them away. No attempt is made here to polish a bevel right to the point or to polish very small flats. The area where the maker's mark is stamped in the blade is also to be avoided in this step because the letters will be washed out by the buff. These problem areas are easily handled in the next step.

Loose buffs are very dangerous if not used correctly and carefully. Beginners should use them with extreme caution. The prime consideration is to hold the blade so that you do not present a point or sharp edge that the buff can grab. An 8-inch buff turning at 3450 rpm can throw a blade with surprising velocity. A knife shop can be a very exciting place at such times.

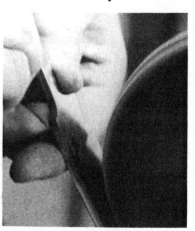

(3) blade polished lengthwise.

143

Step 5 — Grind

"Back to the grinder (blown clean, of course) and a **3M** 600 grit cork-faced belt. This belt is loaded with green chrome rouge so that the abrasive in the cork is scarcely noticed. It would be nice here if 3M made a cork belt free of abrasive for this step. Moderate pressure is used in holding the blade against the wheel. A nice gleam will quickly appear on the blade. If all previous steps have been done correctly, there will be a uniform shine on the blade free of any deep scratches(4).

(4) Correct mirror polishing: a uniform shine, free of deep scratches.

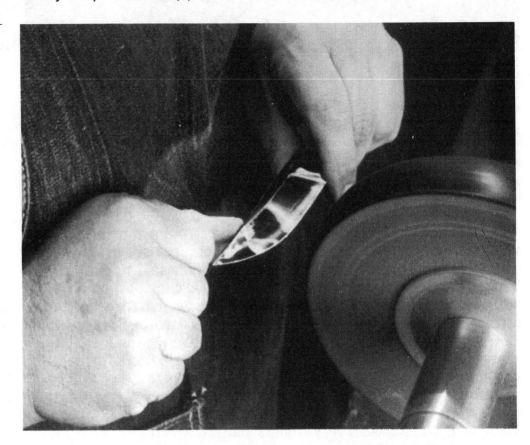

Step 6 — Buff

"The micro scratch pattern from the previous step is removed on an 8x1 loose muslin buff loaded with green chrome rouge. This step will bring up a true mirror finish free of scratches if all previous steps are done correctly. If deep scratches are evident here, go back to the step that seems necessary to remove them and come up through the sequence again. It is futile to try to remove them here. A good light source here is a combination of daylight and fluorescent. Such light will quickly show up any flaws in the finish.

Optional

"An optional step here is to precede the green chrome with Buckeye Products **"Speedie" S-395** (available from Garfield Industries, previously mentioned) on an orange treated loose buff. If step 5 was done correctly this optional step will not be necessary, but the "Speedie" does get rid of scratches quicker than the green chrome alone. If the optional step is used it must be followed by the green chrome to get the desired bright, clear mirror finish."

SECTION IV
THE TOOLS AND
SUPPLIES OF KNIFEMAKING

The object of this book is to help you learn how to make knives, as easily as possible, within the limits of quality and workmanship. So, regardless of what other writers may have said in the past, we consider the handmade knife to be a knife made with tools controlled by human hands alone, rather than by jigs or fixtures. Knifemaking can and should be interesting and enjoyable; to insist, as some purists do, that you should only use files and emery cloth in your knife work is to miss the point of all this.

In this chapter we are going to discuss hand tools and power tools, and how each of the individual tools is used. We've already shown most of these tools in use earlier in the book, and a careful study of the photos will repay you many times over.

The workbench is basic to all other work. It should be strong and rigid, and fastened either to the shop floor or the back wall. Commercial benches made with pressed-steel legs and tops work quite well, if bolted down, but are expensive. The L-shaped bench shown in the Loveless shop is made with 4 x 4 legs, 2 x 4 bracing, and a double layer of 3/4-inch plywood topped with Masonite for the working surface. This bench is larger than you need; a good one-man bench need only be 2 feet from back to front, and 6 feet long. Your local lumber yard can cut the timber to the right lengths, and the parts should be bolted up with 3/8-inch carriage bolts, as shown (1).

Your heavy working vise should be mounted at either front corner of the bench, so that you can swing it and work around all sides of it. We've shown several vises (2), mounted in different positions, but you'll only need one. The **Wilton vise** shown (3) is good but expensive, costing about $90 to $100. A less expensive vise is the European-style unit also shown, available from many tool suppliers for about $40 in the 4-inch size (4).

If you build a backboard on your bench, of 3/4-inch plywood,

(1) The start of a solid workbench.

(2) You'll need a good vise.

146

you'll have a handy place to mount your most-used tools (5). Files, for instance, should never be thrown together in a drawer, but hung individually on nails, to keep them sharp and free of nicks.

(3) The fine Wilton 3-inch vise.

(4) Made in Poland, and under $40!!

(5) Neat and available.

A scriber, a small sharp-pointed tool (6), is used to transfer the knife pattern onto the steel stock. Made either of hardened steel or with a carbide point, this tool is used to draw lines on steel, just as a pencil draws on paper. The hardened steel scriber works well on annealed steel, and is easy to resharpen, but won't mark a heat-treated blade. The carbide scriber will mark just about anything, but is hard to resharpen; you'll need a small diamond file, or a Silicon-Carbide stone.

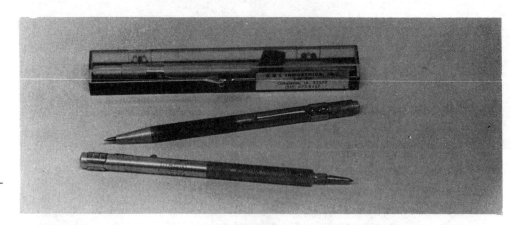

(6) A vital tool, the scriber.

(7) Various kinds of center punches.

Marking the spots on the tang for the handle holes is done with a center punch. This tool is also of hardened steel, and is used only on soft steel, to make a small depression to catch the drill point (7). We like to start the hole with an Automatic Center Punch, and then enlarge it with a regular punch, struck smartly with a hammer.

Get two hammers (8), one with a head weight of about 8 ounces, and a larger one of 32 ounces, for the heavy work. Both should be of the ball-peen type; the smaller rounded end is used for peening work, and should be kept smooth and free of nicks.

The marked and center-punched tang holes can be drilled with a drill press, if you have one, or with a small 1/4-inch hand drill (9). Before hitting the switch, insert the drill point into the

(8) **Typical ball peen hammers.**

(9) **The portable drill in use.**

center-punch mark, and then start slowly, with even pressure on the hand drill. After getting the hole started, get a little oil or cutting lubricant on the drill point; it will cool the drill and make things easier.

A common hacksaw can be used to cut away excess metal from around the pattern. Try to stay as close to the lay-out line as you can without actually touching it, to save labor later on. Keep the cutting action close to the vise, to avoid chatter that would quickly dull the saw blade.

The most efficient way to cut the blade outline is with a metal-cutting bandsaw. These motor-powered units start at about $300 and go up to several thousand; the **POWERMATIC SAW** (10) shown costs about $600. If you get a multiple-speed saw, it can be used to cut handle material and guard stock, by using the higher speed ranges.

The most critically important tool in modern knifemaking is the belt grinder. No other tool in the shop is used as constantly, for so many different jobs, and although knives can be made

(10) **The Powermatic Bandsaw.**

149

without using a belt grinder, the authors know of no successful knifemaker now working who doesn't have some form of this versatile tool in his shop.

The three big names in belt grinding equipment are **BADER, BURR-KING,** and **SQUARE WHEEL.** The Bader Company offers the Bench Model, the **BM-2,** costing about $520, and the much larger **Space Saver,** used mostly in heavy industrial applications costing well over $1,000 when tooled up. The **BM-2** shown is used for all the slack-belt handle shaping in the Loveless shop (11).

The Square Wheel machine is offered in one basic style, using belts from 1-1/2-inches to 4-inches wide, and is the most versatile and easiest-to-set-up of all such grinders now available. The Model 2000, using 2-inch x 72-inch grinding belts, currently costs just under $600, depending on your location freight charges ($567 f.o.b. the plant in Seattle). In some thirteen years of making knives in the Loveless shop, we've never found any job the Square Wheel Model 2000 couldn't handle, quickly and with ease, and we used it exclusively for six years (12).

(11) The Bader belt grinder.

The Burr-King Manufacturing Company in Southern California has listened closely to a few knifemakers in the past three years, and now offers a machine called the **Model 960 Knifemaker's Grinder.** In basic form, equipped with an 8-inch diameter rubber contact wheel (either plain or serrated face), and a platen assembly (13A, 13B), the Model 960 runs about $640, f.o.b. the plant. The Burr-King grinder is extremely smooth and quiet when running, and almost completely free of vibration. Standing in front of a belt grinder for eight hours can make a man count his blessings, and the Burr-King can be called almost pleasant to work with.

(12) The square Wheel belt grinder.

(13A) The Burr-King belt grinder.

(13B) Burr-King's special knifemaker's attachment.

(14) The new Variable Speed D-C Drive Machines.

A recent development of this company is a new Variable-Speed Grinder, using a DC Drive Motor (14). Belt speed on this machine can be slowed down to almost nothing, and it is utilized for slow-speed belt polishing work. Price as of the date of publishing is about $900.

Several smaller belt grinders are on the market, but we do not advise them. A practical alternative is to make your own rig. Here's how to do it: Get one of **BALDOR'S #407B buffers**, and set up the right-hand shaft with a **COSMO** 8-inch contact wheel. The 407B lists for $206, and the **COSMO** wheel for about $55. Then, on the wall behind the machine, mount a **Square Wheel Backstand Idler** unit, spacing it so the combination will accept a standard size abrasive belt, 60-inch or 72-inch, or even longer if you want better results. The Backstand Idler costs $145, so you will end up with a simple belt grinder for well under $450, and still have the left-hand shaft on the Baldor buffer on which to mount your polishing set-up. This set-up does not provide a platen for tang grinding, for instance, but a little ingenuity can fix that. As a matter of fact, this set-up is the most compact and economical one-motor knife shop possible, if you happen to be handy with tools.

The belt grinder uses abrasive belts to do the actual grinding. These belts are (usually) ribbons of a drill cloth coated with a resin on which the abrasive particles are coated. Belts are offered by several national companies; we've used **NORTON, 3M,** and **CLIPPER** belts, made in the USA; and several hundred of the **HERMES** brand belts made in West Germany. They all work pretty well. **NORTON'S NORZON** belts seem to hold up longer than most in rough grinding soft steel, but are a good bit more costly. Clipper belts, made by **SANDPAPER, Inc.,** seem to offer a good balance of cost/working life, and are reasonably priced (15).

(15) The 60-grit, 220-grit, 400-grit, and 500-grit belts.

Sixty grit belts are used to rough the shape of the blade, although some workers go as coarse as 36-grit. The 220-grit belt is then used to clean up the roughed surface, to get ready for heat treatment. For the finishing work, first use a new sharp 220-grit belt, next a 400-grit, and then finish with a dull 500-grit belt, using some kind of belt lubricant like **DYNALENE**. A good beginning order of belts is 100 of the 60-grit, 50 220-grit, 25 400-grit; and 25 of the 500-grit. This quantity will get quite a bit of work done, and will cost about $200 to $250, depending upon source and the quantity discount you get when you order.

Several small hand tools will come in handy, and some are vital. The **Vernier Calipers** shown (16) have been in constant, daily use for about ten years, handling everything from measuring the thickness of bar stock to scribing off lay-out lines. A pair of Micrometers is always useful, but not vital (17), especially for checking the thickness of the blade at various points.

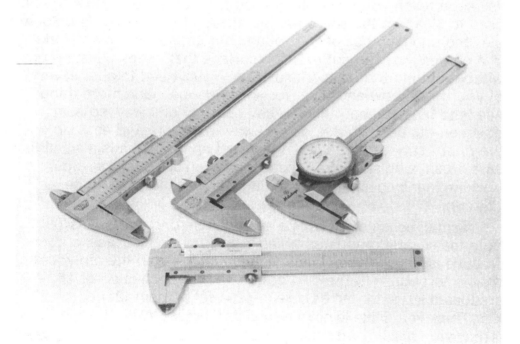

(16) Vernier and Dial Calipers.

And then there are files, dozens of them, all shapes and sizes; seems like you never have enough. They get dull, and must be replaced. Best bet is to contact your local hardware store, get a

(17) Micrometers control your precision work.

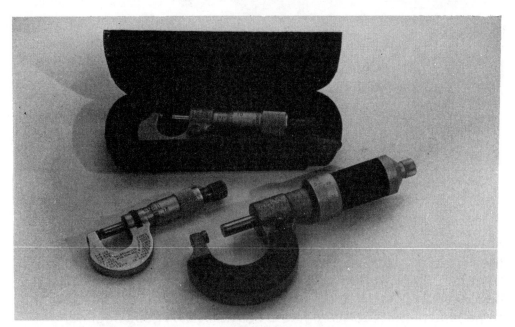

copy of the **SIMMONDS or NICHOLSON File Catalogs,** and look over what is offered. You'll need Flat or Mill files, Taper files, Half-Round files, Square files, Crossing files, and even a little item called a Square Edge Joint File, and all these in assorted lengths and cuts. Files come in three cuts, or degrees of coarseness: the roughest is called Bastard, next is the 2nd cut, and finest of all is the Smooth cut. An 8-inch Mill Smooth file, for instance, is used by Loveless to file the radius just behind the cutting edge that receives the guard. This job could be done by an 8-inch Flat Smooth file, but the Mill file cuts smoother, leaving less finishing work to do.

Note the shapes (18) of the various files shown; experience will soon teach you what files to use for a given job. Note the file used to clean up the soldering job around the guard. It's a Square file, and one face has been ground smooth, so that when working in a corner, you can cut only the surface that needs cleaning up without cutting the adjacent surface. You'll need to alter several of your tools, now and then, for specific jobs. One more thing needs to be said about files. They cut only one way, so bear down on the push stroke, going away from you, and ease up on the return stroke. And keep a file card handy. This is a small flat wire brush, with stiff wire "teeth," and you use it to clean your working file, by pushing and pulling it across the teeth of the file (19).

A small bench block will be useful for setting guard pins (20). Note the several graduated holes in the working surface; a good practice is to use the hole just slightly larger than the pin you are driving through with the drift punch. Drift punches come in graduated sizes, too, so be sure to get a set of them (21).

Think you'd like to have a good drill press? Well, the one shown is made in Taiwan, and usually retails for about $150 (22), including the motor and drill chuck. We list sources later on in the book, by the way, for everything talked about here. And if the lady in your life squawks about money, mention to her that the drill press is very useful around the house, polishing silverware (with a little buffing arbor), repairing furniture, and such like. Fact is, you better get a little practice along these lines in advance, maybe. It helps to stand in front of a mirror while rehearsing what you plan to say, we're told.

(18) A wide variety of files should be available.

(19) Keep your file cleaned constantly.

(20) Setting a guard pin on the bench block.

The drill press is another of those critically important tools the serious knifemaker is going to need, sooner or later. A complete

(21) Drift punches in various sizes.

(22) The drill press is a vital tool.

study of this tool is beyond the scope of the present book, but we suggest you visit your local library, and check out a book on shop technique and shop practice with the drill press. Meanwhile, note the major uses, shown in our photos. Get a press with at least a 1/2-HP motor, and a 1/2-inch drill chuck. Most drill presses provide at least four speeds, usually from about 300 rpm up to about 1800 or 2000 rpm. Some machines have 12 speeds, but that isn't necessary at all; four is enough.

Get some kind of a drill press vise, too, to hold those small parts that need holes, like guards.   Note that we clamp the part in the vise, and with larger drills, always clamp the vise to the drill press table (23).

(23) Best quality drill press vises.

A small tool called a countersink, or c'sink (24), is used to break the corner of the hole before heat-treating the blade; this is called chamfering the hole, and is a must, to keep small cracks from forming around the hole when the blade is being quenched to harden it. Run the tool dead slow and lightly cut the hole edges, just breaking the corner.

(24) Various hand and machine countersinks.

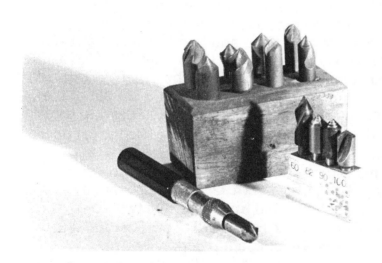

The small drills used to drill holes, on the drill press or with a hand drill, are called drill bits, and sometimes twist drills. The class of drills you'll need are called High Speed (the kind of steel they are made of) Straight Shank (as opposed to Taper Shank, used in some machines) drills. In the tool catalogs, you'll sometimes see that abbreviated as H.S.S.S. drills. They come graduated in fractional sizes and number sizes (25), ranging from 1/16-inch up to 1/2-inch in diameter for the fractionals, and from #1 (.228-inch in diameter) down to #60 (.040-inch). There are even smaller ones, from #61 to #80, but you'll have no use for these little drills untill much farther along in your work. If you have a choice, buy the Cobalt grade, which stay sharp much longer than the regular High Speed grade.

In Section II, Chapter 1, ''How To Make A Knife By The Stock Removal Method,'' we showed certain lay-out work being done on a granite Surface Plate with a precision tool called a **Height Gauge.** We don't feel such equipment is vital, but it will help you control your lay-out lines and dimensions very closely. These items are sold by machinist's supply houses and machine shop supply dealers in all large cities.

(25) **A complete assortment of H.S.S.S. drills, from #80 to 1/2-inch.**

You are going to need pliers, in several types and sizes (26). You'll use them to hold small pins and parts, and to clamp up handle assemblies during drilling and handle fitting, and after assembly, while the epoxy is setting up. The Bent Long Nose, the Parallel Jaw, the Kleins, the Vise Grips, and the Lever Wrench all will get a lot of use in the knife shop. Note that a couple of the tools are actually clamps in the form of pliers, and used to grip thicker work. The **STARRETT #1 Cut Nippers** are used to cut guard pins, and do a dandy job (27).

You'll need some form of heat source for guard soldering. The large electric soldering iron shown (28) will work, but even better is an oxy-acetylene torch, fed from the usual twin-tank set-up (29). The small hand set is called a **LITTLE TORCH**, and is available through the usual welding shop supply house.

Using the #5 tip with the Little Torch provides an intense but compact flame for the guard soldering job shown in Section II, Chapter 1. Special low-pressure gauges furnished by the **Smith Welding Equipment Division of Tescom Corporation** should be used with Little Torch, to exactly regulate the gas flow through the handpiece. The tool shown has been in constant use for over ten years. None of the tips has ever burnt out, nor have the gauges ever needed rebuilding. Another small hand torch is available, but doesn't have the ruby tips used on the Little Torch and can't be expected to last nearly as long (30).

(26) Several different pliers and cutters.

(27) Cutting a guard pin.

(28) A large electric soldering iron.

(29) **The basic oxy-acetylene outfit: tanks, gauges, torch.**

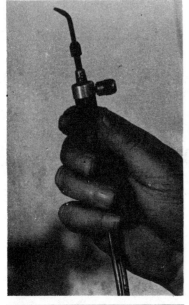

(30) **A good answer, the Little Torch.**

A larger oxy-acetylene outfit can be used, of course. Some units now on the market include a handpiece, tips, gauges, and hose, ready to hook up to tanks, which can be rented from the supplier quite reasonably. Lately, the shop has acquired a portable Spot Welder imported from Monaco, a small country in the south of France (31). This unit is hand-held, and is used a great deal in the mobile home industry. We are using it to rapidly heat the stainless steel guard soldering job, to provide a completely clean source of heat (the major problem in mounting stainless guards is soldering; and dirt in the joint will prevent a saturated joint). This is still an experimental technique, but so far, shows great promise on this difficult job.

We've already covered the use of the one kind of coated abrasive product, the grinding belts used on the belt grinder. But when it's time to start shaping up the knife handle, you'll need several grits of a product called a Bench Roll (32). These are available from all the major abrasives companies in widths from 1/2-inch to 3-inches, usually in a standard length of 50 yards. Grits range from 24 to 500, but you'll need only three at the most: the 240 grit, 320 grit, and 500 grit. Buy the 1-inch x 50-yard rolls, and then tear the strip down the center when you need a narrower width.

Well, now, you say you've got a bench grinder out in the garage, and what can you do with it? Fact is, not too much. You can grind the outline of your blade with it, and you can grind the bevels, if you're careful. We've never had much luck trying to make a knife on such a rig, and started out using a belt grinder, a **HAMMOND VH-2d,** some twenty-three years ago. We don't like the results of using the hard clay vitrified wheels used on bench grinders; when grinding the blade bevel, for instance, we suspect such wheels leave small, microscopic bits of silica imbedded in the surface of the steel, and such minute particles cannot be beneficial to the results of heat treatment. Another objection is that a clay wheel seems to bounce the work badly during free-hand grinding, and soon gets out of dynamic running balance,

(31) **The portable spot welder.**

160

resulting in a high-frequency running impact, a hammering action, that coincides with the turning speed, usually 3450 rpm, of the wheel. The large slow wheels used by a few companies in the commercial cutlery business work differently, with very slow rim speeds, but even this practice is rapidly dying out.

But if you happen to have a bench grinder with a 5/8-inch—11 tpi threaded shaft end, you can do this: buy one of the back-up discs used in the auto body shops, mount it on your shaft end, with a fitted round abrasive disc, and then grind bevels with it. Such a set-up is good for rough grinding, but you'll still need to finish off the blade with drawing-filing (to clean up and flatten the bevels) and emery polishing, with a piece of bench roll.

(32) **Bench rolls above the workbench.**

One form of grinder that is very useful is the little hand-held electric high-speed tool typified by the **Dremel Moto-tool.** The photo shows three different forms of such tools (33). These small rotary tools, turning at 35,000 rpm, are very useful for getting into tight places in handle forming, carving, spot polishing, and inletting nameplates on knife handles.

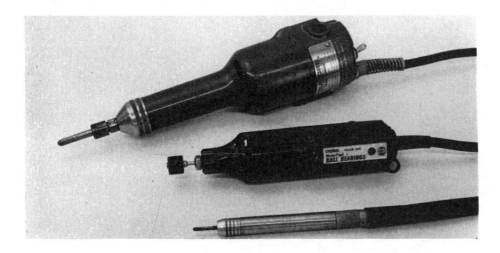

(33) **Three kinds of rotary power tools.**

Small drum sanders can be mounted in the drill press spindle, and used to grind and clean up finger grooves. Numerous other small accessories can be used on most shop power tools, and are sometimes worth their cost.

A very useful addition to the drill press is the rig called the **Dual Cross Slide Milling Table,** also called a **Universal Compound Table,** which is mounted directly to the drill press table and holds a vise, usually a common Drill Press Vise, which in turn holds the work. This kind of set-up is used for very light milling work, such as opening up the slot, or hole, in a fighting knife guard. In use, you make a series of small holes with a drill bit, and then carefully mill out the webs between the holes, using a suitable end mill mounted in the chuck of the drill press. Drill press bearings cannot handle radial loads very well, so this kind of rig is used only for very light work.

There is more than one way to do almost every job in making a knife. The tools we have described are typical, but as you accumulate experience, you'll quickly learn other ways to do things besides those we have shown in this book. No man can claim to know everything about knifemaking, and more is being learned every year. Accept what we have shown as a starting point, and go on to find your own special little short cuts and methods. Your tools will play a large part in everything you do, and some of the tools you buy will end up lasting for years. It will pay you to choose carefully, and buy the best quality you can afford, because nothing will discourage you more than poor quality working tools. Buy wisely, and then take good care of your equipment.

First let's discuss the steel; and if you've been following this business of making handmade knives for very long, you probably know by now that there are several different grades of tool steel suitable for good blades. It seems that each well-known knifemaker has his own favorite grade of steel, and it's easy to get confused about the subject. But don't let your own work be influenced by all the noise and confusion. Once you've gotten your equipment set up, your first job is to build up your working skills; learning how to hold the steel to the grinder, and how to shape it, and then polish it, and so forth.

So you will need a steel that is easy to obtain and to work with, and that, frankly, means the grade called 0-1, an oil-hardening tool steel offered by just about any machine-shop supply company anywhere. You can buy it by the piece, one piece at a time, by asking the man for 0-1 Flat Ground Stock. Want to start with a nice little 4-inch hunting knife? Just get a chunk 3/16 inch x 1-1/4 inches x 18 inches, which is the standard length it comes in. Or how about a penknife blade? Ask for a piece 1/16 inch x 1/2 inch x 18 inches. The point is, 0-1 stock comes in a wide range of sizes, is widely distributed throughout the country by several steel companies, and it makes up into a very good knife. Brown & Sharpe even furnishes it with the lay-out color pre-coated, a nice dark blue, in a grade called **READY MARK.**

0-1 tool steel, in Flat Ground Stock form, is spheroidized annealed. This simply means that it is very soft and easy to work with, as tool steels go. It cuts easily with a hacksaw, and compared to other knife steels it grinds like butter. Yet, it makes up into a very good knife, with good working toughness and edge-holding properties. It heat-treats easily, and if you don't care to try it yourself, most any heat-treating shop in the country will know how to handle it (just tell the man to draw it to RC 58-59). We would be misleading you if we said that 0-1 will make a knife of the very best quality, because it won't; several other grades do better. But these other grades are often much harder to work with, requiring complicated heat treatment after a good deal more work in the shop, and the difference is not as great as you might think. After you have acquired experience with your tools, made several knives, and learned how to judge the quality of your finished work, then is the time to begin thinking about better steels.

(This subject of blade steels will be discussed more thoroughly in follow-up articles, to be published from time to time in the AMERICAN BLADE MAGAZINE. Later these articles will be collated into another book on advanced knifemaking.)

You are going to want to fit something between the blade of your knife, and the handle, if for no other reason than to protect your fingers. This little bit of metal is called a guard by some, and by others a hilt. No matter what you decide to call it, make it out of brass on your first go-around. A brass guard is traditional, for a good reason: brass is easy to get, and easy to work with. The yellow color is attractive, and a guard made of full-hard brass will last as long as the knife does. Later, after you've gotten into things a bit, you'll want to try a guard of nickel silver, a beautiful metal almost white in color, but which is a good deal more difficult to work with. Finally, you may want to try a guard of stainless steel, maybe on a 440C blade, and you'll have your work cut out for you; we can think of nothing more challenging than trying to get a good solder joint with a 440C blade and a guard of Grade 303 stainless steel. Here's a tip: make your guard of Grade 416 stainless, and use **Eutectic's 157B solder.** Preheat carefully, keeping the joint clean; and praying helps a little, too, if you can remember the words.

Now let's consider handle materials, and what you decide to use for your knife handle will determine to a great degree just how nice your knife looks. This discussion of handle materials will begin with the stuff called Sambar stag, the animal horn imported from India by two or three suppliers. When used by a skilled knifemaker who has carefully chosen his handle piece for color, shape, and surface pattern, a knife handle of Sambar stag is thought by most people to be the most attractive of all materials.

One of your authors has been making full-tanged knives exclusively for about ten years, and stag handles are requested by more than half of his customers. We've spent hundreds of hours laying stag slabs out on a large table under strong light, trying to grade for color and shape and pattern. This backlog of experience has been costly, and led to one definite conclusion: knife handles of Sambar stag will gradually become more and more rare, if present trends continue. In just the last five years, Sambar stag has increased four hundred percent in price, from about $2 a pair (of slabs) to $8 at the time of writing this book. During that period, the quality has gone down: the very finest stag is rarely available now. Perhaps in time it will disappear from the market. We've heard rumors that certain German cutlery companies have warehouses full of the stuff, but we have not heard of any large supply stocks currently available in the United States.

Another point should be made about stag knife handles. The serious knifemaker should be concerned with how well the knife handle fits the hand. To get a good fit, by shaping the handle to fit the working hand, often means having to grind away much of the surface of the stag. Thus, you end up literally throwing away the very qualities you chose the stag for in the first place.

One final point should be made about stag handles: during the past two decades, we've examined a great many very old knives, some of them made in the early years of the nineteenth century. Without exception, the old knives made with stag handles were in very poor condition. The handles were usually cracked, and often badly shrunk away from the steel, with the handle sometimes even being loose on the tang. We've noted this condition even on knives made during the 1940s and early 1950s, which were brought into the shop to have new handles fitted.

So we are not as impressed by stag handles as we used to be.

And we feel much the same way about most of the other so-called "natural" materials used for knife handles: tusk ivory is notorious for cracking and shrinking, as is hippo tooth ivory and walrus ivory. Indeed, ivory handles look very beautiful, at first, but require constant care. Taking an ivory-handled hunter from the outside cold of a winter hunting trip into a warm room is asking for trouble. Several makers no longer offer ivory handles at all, and the New York ivory market seems to offer only poacher tusk now, green ivory that often cracks or splits before you can get it cut into handle-sized blocks.

Consider the various hardwoods traditionally used by knifemakers, such as ebony (either Gaboon or Macassar), cocobolo, padouk, teak, bubinga, zebrawood, tulipwood, and East Indian satinwood, to name only a few. There are literally dozens of such hardwoods, either native or imported, that can be used for knife handles. All are prone to cracking, and require careful handling in the shop. These materials should be aged for several months, after being cut into handle-size blocks, before being finally fitted and assembled on a finished knife.

Consider the experience of a fellow we know well, a former student in our shop. In early 1976 he spent several dozen hours building a very fine replica Bowie knife. He'd hand-finished his blade to a very fine satin finish, and fitted a solid silver guard, butt cap, and handle nameplate. The work was truly outstanding, a fine example of what can be done by a dedicated amateur knifemaker. He brought the knife into the shop, took it out of the case, handed it to us, and asked what could be done. The Gaboon ebony handle had cracked, right from the guard up the handle to the butt, and opened up a good 1/8 inch, right down to the tang. And all this after he had aged the ebony for eighteen months before mounting it. We suggested rebuilding with **Micarta**, which is what he ended up doing.

The point, of course, is that one aspect of making a fine knife is being able to predict a long and useful life for it. You can see why we don't feel so good any more about using any of the "natural" materials on a knife we hope will be working away, thirty or even fifty years from now.

What else is left? If we eliminate those materials that are prone to premature failure, what can we use for good knife handles? Well, quite a few materials are around. During the middle 1960s we made quite a few knife handles out of a material called **Benelex**, which was nothing but a very high grade of **Masonite**, the stuff you can buy in any lumber yard. Those knives are still around, and still working fine; no cracks and no shrinkage, and with a nice patina of age and use on the handles. During the mid-1950s, we made several knife handles out of block nylon obtained from a plastics supplier. Some we dyed (with **Rit** fabric dye, on the top of the kitchen stove) a bright orange; the customer had trouble mislaying his knives in hunting camp, and that color job cured the problem fine. Block nylon is still available, and still expensive, but makes a knife handle with no known limit to its working lifetime.

Or consider the handle material many working knifemakers are using now, the phenolic resin laminate called Micarta. It comes in several colors and grades, is easy to work with, and has no known limit to its working life. The genuine stuff is made only by Westinghouse (GE makes a similar material, but doesn't call it Micarta). It comes in natural tan, dark red, dark green, and black, all laminated in fine-weave linen. The 400 grade Micarta, a coarse canvas-phenolic laminate in forest green color, is especially good for working field knives. There is also a material that nicely replaces tusk ivory, called Ivory Micarta, or sometimes White, or Bone, Micarta. It isn't a phenolic material, but is a laminate of epoxy and white paper. Ivory Micarta is very popular with many knife buyers, users and collectors alike and, like the various Micartas, is available in several basic sizes at reasonable cost.

Thus, there are several good materials available for working knife handles. Although some purists object to them because they are man-made, or because they ''look like plastic'' or are not traditional, once you have put a knife together with something like this, you can do a fine job of shaping the handle to suit you, and also can be confident that it will last far longer than your lifetime.

Finally, as you progress in your own knifemaking, you'll have plenty of chances to use your own ingenuity. Fellow came into the shop a few weeks back with an old double-bitted lumberman's axe. Said it had belonged to his granddad, who had used it in Upper Michigan, and could we use part of the hickory handle for his Dropped Hunter, which we were getting ready to finish. We looked it over, said ''Sure,'' and a week or so later, sent him away happy as a pup with a new bone. So we started thinking, and are going to use some more hickory, pretty soon, because straight-grained second-growth hickory is really pretty sound stuff. It doesn't seem to want to crack much, and takes a nice stain, if you want to color it. The American hardwood known as Osage orange is another wood worth trying. It used to be found on good bows. The scientific name is ''Maclura pomifera,'' and it's available from dealers in hardwoods. Several other domestic hardwoods, such as black locust (''Robinia pseudoacacia''), blue gum (''Eucalyptus globulus''), and sweet birch (''Betula lenta''), bear looking into, because of their high strength and density, although we've had no direct experience yet with them.

So look around you, pick something that looks right, and try putting a knife together with it. If it doesn't work, you can always tear it apart, and rebuild with something else. And you will be learning as you go, and that's the name of that tune.

Finally, consult Chapter 4 in this section, on ''Sources of Services and Materials,'' for where to get all this stuff.

This is a book on knifemaking and the tools, the materials and the methods used. The greatest living knifemakers have tried and tested everything we discuss here. Individuals all, each of the American custom knifemakers will set up his shop to suit himself and will use the materials in somewhat different ways. But in general, we have presented an accurate guide that will serve the reader well.

If the reader follows directions closely there is little excuse for failure. It goes without saying that there is no other way to gain the skills necessary than to make knives, many of them. The beginner is bound to make mistakes, and those too should be considered part of the learning process. With time, practice and determination the once fumble-fingered novice will be able to produce well-made, perfectly acceptable knives.

But how will they look? Chances are good that they will look something like a Loveless, or a Moran or some other well-known knifemaker's work. In the beginning, there isn't really anything wrong with that and it may be the safest way to go. After all, the way the American custom knife looks, feels and performs is probably the reason that you want to learn to make knives.

Just what is it that gives the custom knife that special quality, that certain look and feel? Let's go back a bit. The explosive renaissance of handmade or custom knives is less than a decade old and yet, in the opinion of the authors, archetypes have emerged and even the dim beginnings of various schools seem to be forming.

The first major designer of knives in modern times was Bo Randall. A comparison of Randall knives with those of Bill Scagel indicates Randall's early love affair with the look of that old maker's knives. (See Section I, Chapter 1, ''A History of Handmade Knives,'' for pictures.) It was Randall who showed the world what a good, handmade knife could be and early on, his catalogs and the pictures that appeared in magazines of the Randall knife were literally the only source of visual information. Many, if not most, of the early makers patterned their knives after the Randall. That influence can't ever be denied. It is historical fact.

One man's fame and another man's discontent with his own copying led to the development of the most powerful design influence in knifemaking today. R.W. Loveless has put his mark on not only the rather limited world of the custom makers but has also forced a large segment of the commercial cutlers to take a long, hard look at their own old, tired designs. A few of the more progressive have introduced new and superior lines, many showing more than a little of the Loveless ''touch.''

Loveless' design influence lays heavily on knives known as "using" knives, the hunters' and the fighting knives. To imply that his is the ''alpha'' and the ''omega'' of all knife design would be misleading. Others have gone their own conceptual directions and their influence is strong.

The state of Utah has produced more than its share of

knifemakers and the way that these knives look has contributed heavily to the "period" or "Art" blades so popular among many collectors today.

Speaking rather loosely, the "Utah" school of makers was birthed by a man named Gil Hibben. He was one of the first workers in the steel called 440C and his early knives were forged out of that material. He was one of the first to build "classic" Bowies, daggers and short swords. Hibben trained a man named Harvey Draper in his shop and later Draper opened his own knife business. He made the Utah style of hunting knife with the upswept blade, but also carried on with the "traditional" heavy blades of the past, doing a better job than his teacher. He was one of the first to make decorative guards and pommels, and his finish was, for a time, the best in the country.

One day an intense but likable man brought some of his knives to Draper's shop for appraisal. Later, Buster Warenski stayed on and worked side by side with Draper developing the highly skilled grinding art that is characteristic of the Utah makers.

About the same time, a displaced Alaskan Indian with highly developed artistic skills came to the Draper shop and spent a very concentrated period of time learning knifemaking skills. This man, Rod Chappel, returned to his home in Spokane, Washington and proceeded to add a completely new look to knives with his highly sculptured blades and radical handles.

Both Buster Warenski and Rod Chappel have added new depths and heights to custom knifemaking, and anyone who would know about knives should make a complete study of their work.

Nor can the reader fail to study the knives of another of those makers who stand more or less alone. Lloyd Hale, of Springdale, Arkansas has taken the "Art" blade to new places and his decorative blades have had a deep influence on many makers.

No discussion of the way knives look could be comprehensive without the listing of D. E. Henry. This man's knives represent an element of design that might be called purity. He has taken elements of the English-style Bowie and refined every detail until the Henry Bowie stands alone in its pure essence. In the opinion of the authors, no other maker has yet duplicated the "look" of a Henry knife, and some very highly skilled craftsmen have tried. Henry's workmanship and styling have set standards so high that many makers look to his knives as a sort of goal to strive for. He is one of the true archetypes.

Featured in this book is William F. Moran, of Frederick, Maryland. We have shown, step by step, how he makes his knives. In Section I, Chapter 1, you will find a display of his work that was made some fifteen years ago. These knives are uniquely Moran, as are the knives he makes today. Moran himself will freely admit that many late makers produce finer finishes, closer fits and "slicker" work. But, like the other men listed in this chapter, his work is unmistakably HIS. Looking at and hefting a Moran knife instantly connects the sensitive person with some other age. Moran cannot make a "modern" knife, and he says so. His recent fame as the first American to make "Damascus" steel is well deserved, but to this author his uncanny ability to touch man's own history in his knife design is equally important to any student of contemporary knives.

One of the voids in custom knifemaking today is at the low-priced end. For the reader who may want to investigate this wide-open area, there are no better knife designs to study than those of Harvey Morseth. Although he is long gone to his reward, his designs live on in the Morseth line as advertised and sold by the present owner of Morseth knives, A. G. Russell of Springdale, Arkansas. What the reader should study is the simple efficiency of the design, the complete usefulness, the thin blade, and the functional handle. By no means be content with copying. Rather, look carefully for the essence of the knife and then strike out on your own. Harry Morseth made a knife to be used hard without a lot of frills. The market just may be wide open for such a knife today.

The men mentioned above are those who this author considers important in the area of design and as pacesetters in that area. It does not necessarily follow that they make the best knives around. Dozens of current makers produce superb knives, and the aspiring knifemaker must get every catalog of every maker he can. No other single act can help so much in learning knife design.

The designing of knives is so personal and so subjective that very little can be taught in the conventional sense of the word.

A few pointers may be of help. Foremost in the authors' opinion is always the question, "Will the knife function as designed for the purpose intended?" Obviously we are not talking about minimums here. It's possible to gut a deer with a penknife, and some enemy sentry can be dispatched quite well with a fifty-cent ice pick. In the context of this book, function means not just well but superbly.

A remark by R. W. Loveless has real meaning to the maker who would earn his daily bread by making knives. "A knife must not only be made from the best steel available, the best handle material, and the best construction possible, but it must also have visual and tactical appeal so that the customer will just have to pick it up, fall in love with the feel of it, and maybe buy it."

It is extremely important in knife design to have or develop the ability to put your ideas about knife design on paper.

There is no other practical way for the knifemaker to see his ideas develop, to make changes, and to visually appraise his efforts. By making overlays, subtle line changes can be made, shifted slightly, widened, shortened, narrowed, etc. If you think you can't draw, practice until you can.

The following photographs will show how some different knifemakers have approached the same kind of a knife. In this case, it is the fighting knife or the combat knife. They range in size from the 8-1/2 inch Loveless Big Bear to the little Gerber Mark I

Boot knife. Makers give these weapons different names, but it amounts to little more than semantics.

The most famous fighting knife, and the one that has been around the longest, is the Randall #1 (1). Its 8-inch blade is described as an "all purpose fighting knife." It has enough point for penetration and the top front clip can be sharpened.

(1) The Randall #1. One of the oldest, still one of the best.

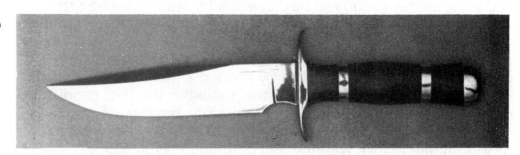

Rod Chappel's Hunting Leopard combat knife has a massive guard, a clipped point that is hollow ground and sharp, and is designed to use either edge up or down (2).

(2) The giant Chappel Hunting Leopard.

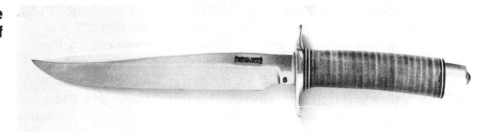

Dwight Towell's Bowie-style fighting knife is a neat and straightforward blade with a false clipped edge (3).

(3) Towell's approach to the neat knife.

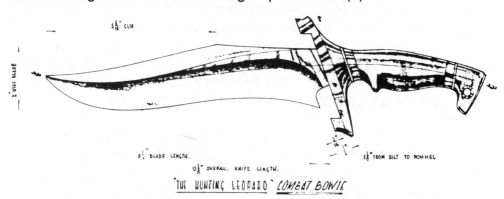

Illustrated, is a hollow ground Bowie type built by "Kuzan" Oda, partner in the Loveless shop, and is lighter than it looks, with a thin blade and a wide but comfortable grip (4).

(4) A lightweight design by Oda.

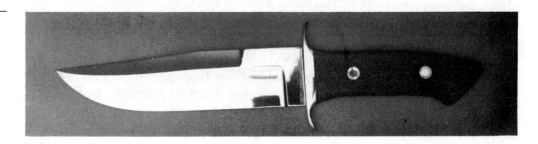

The Gerber Mark 2 is generally a dagger with a long blade that has serrations near the guard. It is made of good tool steel and comes very sharp(5).

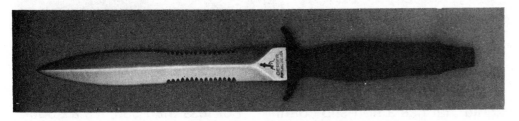

(5) The Mark 2 Gerber.

These two Loveless knives are unusual. The one with the aluminum alloy butt (6) is a Delaware maid and dates back to 1957. The other is the current fighting knife as made in the Loveless shop (7). It shows the dramatic change that took place first in the maker's mind, then on paper, and finally in steel. Of

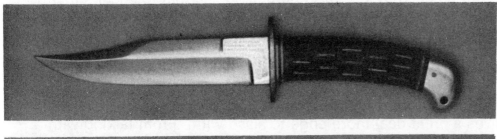

(6,7) The strong Loveless knives show the changes from the late 1950s (aluminum butt) to the current model.

course, the big knife is the famed Loveless Big Bear, an awesome weapon and probably the most expensive undecorated fighting knife in the world (8).

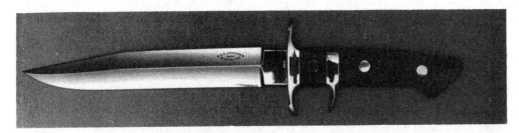

(8) The famous Loveless BIG BEAR.

Blackie Collins' all steel combat knife is a broad double-edged dagger type with plenty of weight but somewhat blunt (9).

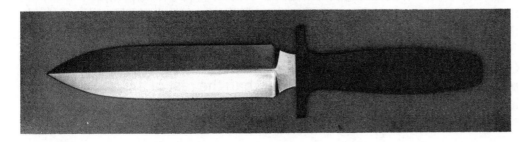

(9) Blackie Collins' approach is an all steel design.

(10) The Mark 1 Gerber Boot Knife.

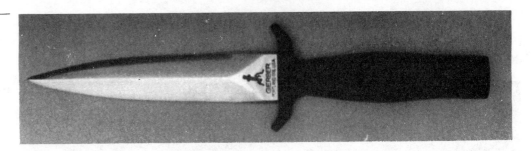

The Mark 1 Gerber is a short little boot knife with an alloy handle that has a non-slip coating . For less than $35, it's a good buy (10).

Each maker has his own ideas about knives in general. Here are a few remarks about fighting knives by three makers:

MORAN: "There is a type of thing we call a combat knife today — it's probably a pretty small knife — the type of thing that might be used by the CIA and people like that to sneak up and stab somebody or some other undercover kind of thing. But back in World War II, when a soldier would actually face another man with a knife in actual combat, he wanted a great big knife, a slashing weapon — it had psychological value along with it. So the concept of combat knives is completely different today than what it was during World War II. The high point (on his knife) gives a great deal more edge to slash with. From talking with guys that have used a knife it's more important to cut the guy than stick him.''

LOVELESS: "I think the diamond shape, double hollow ground blade is a very dramatic looking kind of thing, but aside from that it is very strong for the weight it uses. You don't end up with a great big heavy kind of a knife. It is almost like a surgical instrument. It is an extremely efficient way to use a certain weight of knife — they are light for their reach and make a very fast knife in action and high motion speeds, and quick motions in knife fighting definitely have some value. The double hollow grind gives you a knife that you can plunge all the way into something very easily. One thing I always insisted on is that the top front cutting edge be just as truly functional as the bottom cutting edge, and the hollow grind is a way to get there."

ROD CHAPPEL: "My designs of combat Bowies or combat fighting knives hinge around mobility, flexibility, at least two cutting edges, and the fact that the knife must be strong enough to withstand pressures and stresses above the standard hunting or utility knife. I thought that the theme of my combat blade should be something that is familiar to the American fighting man (the Bowie). I have incorporated three major changes. The first is the top clip, which is hollow ground so that the cutting edge, even when dull, will cut, and the hollow grind runs the full length of the top of the cutting edge. Second, the bottom cutting edge strongly resembles the Military Gurkha Kukri knife that is used in India. Third, the area around the pointing finger and thumb is thinner than the rest of the handle and it is emphasized by a finger hold for extra stability in the preference of style the man chooses to fight with."

These three men have three somewhat different ideas about the "best" fighting knife. Although different, each style has those customers who consider themselves lucky to have such a blade.

As many or more variations exist in the design of the American "hunting knife." The photographs that follow are only a small sampling of what is available.

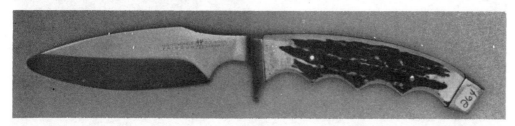

(11) **The German-made Henckel's hunter.**

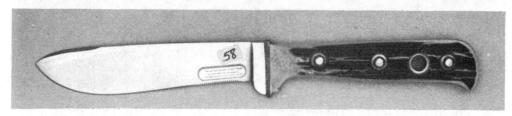

(12) **Puma's Hunting Pal, another German design.**

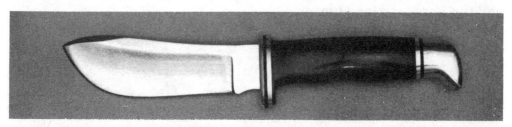

(13) **The Buck Skinner.**

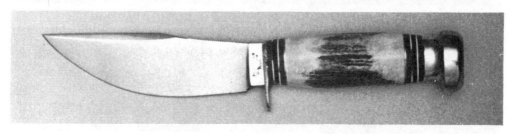

(14) **Marble's Woodcraftsman, a noted design from the 1930s.**

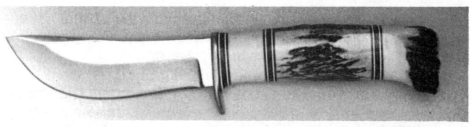

(15) **A current Morseth Cascade Skinner.**

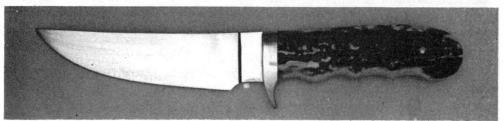

(16) **Barney's copy of a D. E. Henry hunter.**

Any of these knives will serve as a hunting knife, some better than others. Aside from any consideration of construction, materials, etc., there are some interesting design features. The Gerber Magnum hunter and the Flayer are knives that have been in the line for a considerable time.

(17) The big Gerber Magnum, from the 1950s, with handle design by Thomas Lamb.

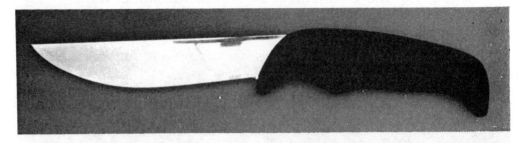

(18) A Gerber skinner from the 1960s.

The latest Gerber designs are represented by the Drop Point and the Presentation Hunter.

(19) A late effort from Gerber's designer Al Mar, the C-325 dropped hunter.

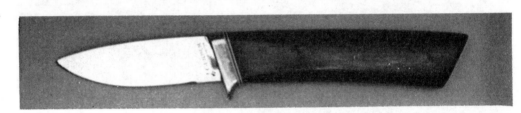

(20) Pete Gerber's Presentation Hunter.

The changes are obvious. What is not obvious is that Gerber has expended great effort and considerable money to upgrade their products. Many other cutlery firms have not.

The German knives have a definite old European look. The old Marble's was well-known to thousands of Boy Scouts and was (and is) a very good knife in the woods. The Morseth three-piece stag Cascade Skinner is an older knife but the same knife is still available from A. G. Russell Company and is as good today as when Harry Morseth designed it.

The best advice for the beginner in knifemaking is to send (with the right amount of money) for every knife catalog you can. Note what you like and dislike. If you have the opportunity (and if you're dead serious, you"ll make the opportunity) go to a knife show or a show where knives will be displayed. Look them over carefully, and ask to handle them. Note again what is "right" for you.

(21) A hunter from Joe Cordova of Albuquerque.

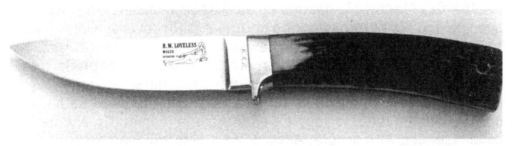

(22) A rare Loveless narrow tang Banana Skinner.

(23) The classic Loveless Dropped Hunter.

Then make knives, all kinds of knives. Work until you know your tools and your skills have developed a sense of confidence that says "I can do anything."

Whether you intend to make one knife or a great many, the look and feel of the knife that is your creation is of utmost importance.

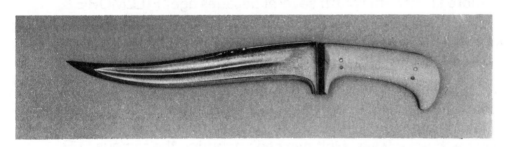

(24) A rare and beautiful Persian dagger.

Just in case you feel that everything has been done in the field of knives and there just isn't any place for the new man to go, photo 24 is included. It is an old Persian fighting knife made of ivory and the real Damascus steel. It has a beauty of its own, and more important to us is the fact that there isn't a maker around today who could make it. So if you ever get down in the mouth about "nothing left to do," go to a good museum in a large city and view what the ancients did. It will open your eyes and give you hope.

We don't intend this to be an all-inclusive listing of the places where you can get everything you'll need for making knives; that's a tall order, and space is limited. So we are listing here only those sources we have personal knowledge of, companies we have dealt with and found to be reputable and trustworthy.

CUSTOM KNIFEMAKER'S SUPPLY, P.O. Box 308, Emory, TX 75440. This outfit is headed up by Bob Schrimsher, who has been selling supplies to working knifemakrs for several years now, ever since the late 1960s, when he went into the game full-time. Sells steel, brass and nickel silver, Stag, Micarta, ready-made blades and guards, etc., and belt grinding machines and other equipment. Send him a dollar for a catalog, and then wait patiently until he can get it out to you; it's almost a one-man outfit, and he is usually loaded with orders. A fine fellow, who will lean over backwards to please.

ANGUS-CAMPBELL, INCORPORATED, 4417 South Soto Street, Los Angeles, CA 90058. Ken Campbell offers just about every kind of man-made handle material known, along with epoxies and quick-bond adhesives. Minimum order is $10, and Ken offers one-day shipment on new orders; a price list is available, on request. This shop is a leading supplier of Micarta material.

FILLMORE & GARBER, INCORPORATED, 1742 Floradale Ave., South El Monte, CA 91733. Tom Newton heads up a good crew here, specializing in abrasive supplies and equipment. Sells Square-Wheel and Burr-King belt grinders, and stocks a big assortment of all grades of grinding belts. Ever since Millard Fillmore started this outfit several decades ago, FILLMORE & GARBER has been a leading industrial abrasives supplier in Southern California, handling major accounts all over the West. Outstanding, next-day service, too.

PACIFIC HEAT TREATING COMPANY, 1238 Birchwood Drive, Sunnyvale, CA 94086. Billy Holt is the boss-man here, and we know of no man more dedicated to fine and careful handling of your work than he. If we say Mr. Holt has been handling the famous D.E. Henry Bowie blades for ten years or more, little more needs be added. There's a shop minimum charge of $35, and this outfit specializes in the hard-to-handle alloys. When you get into 154CM blades, for instance, a dozen at a time, this is the place to go. Billy has the technical background to work with the newer steels, and his facilities include a fine and up-to-date test lab.

Several other firms and companies offer services and/or supplies to knifemakers, and we include them here:

ATLANTA CUTLERY CORPORATION, Box 33266, Decatur, GA 30033. Bill Adams is well known in knife circles, and is now offering blades and handle materials. Send $1 for their catalog.

BARTLETT & CO., INC., 5 South Wabash Avenue, Chicago, IL 60603. Catalog $1; tools, polishing supplies and equipment, engraving supplies.

BROWNELLS INC., Rt. 2, Box 1, Montezuma, IA 50171. Phone (515) 623-5401. Tools, heat-treat furnace, polishing supplies.

PAUL H. GESSWEIN & CO., 235 Park Avenue South, New York, NY 10003. Phone (212) 982-2265. Fine files, hand grinders, burrs, felt wheels, etc.

GOLDEN AGE ARMS COMPANY, Box 283, Delaware, OH 43015. Offers a general assortment of knifemaking supplies, along with Sambar stag.

HAUNI RICHMOND, INCORPORATED, 5100 Charles City Road, Richmond, VA 23231. This company offers vacuum heat-treating and metallurgical consulting on the more complex alloy grades, and comes highly recommended. They suggest sending a sketch of your work, listing grades and quantities, for their quote.

INDIAN RIDGE TRADERS, P.O. Box 20039, Ferndale, MI 48220. Long a supplier of English-made finished blades; offering other supplies as well.

INDUSTRIAL PIPE AND STEEL, 9936 Rush Street, South El Monte, CA 91733. Phone (213) 443-9467. Free catalog; tools, drill presses, milling machines, vises, etc.

OLYMPIC EQUIPMENT, Box 80187, Seattle, Washington 98108. The manufacturer of the Square Wheel Grinder. Because of continued improvements, contact them for information on their tools.

R & W CUTLERY SUPPLY, Box 620, San Rafael, CA 94901. Offers steel, handle materials, heat-treating, etc.

L. SHOR CO., INC., 71 Fifth Avenue, NY 10003. Phone (212) 924-2200. Small tools, files etc.; catalog $1.

SILVO HARDWARE CO., 107-109 Walnut Street, Philadelphia, PA 19106. Tools, catalog $1.

SWEST INC., 10803 Composite Drive, Dallas, TX 75220. Phone (214) 350-4011. Catalog $1; tools, equipment, precious metals, polishing equipment.

In addition to the sources listed, every edition of the AMERICAN BLADE MAGAZINE carries display advertising for companies offering supplies and services for knifemakers. If you don't already subscribe, do so as soon as possible. This isn't merely a "house plug," either. There simply isn't any other publication which follows the handmade knife scene so completely, and you'll get some useful information out of every issue.

One further publication will be very helpful: the classified telephone directory for the nearest large city. You can get these from your local phone company, and find the nearest sources for shop supplies, steel, handle materials (look under "Plastics"), or whatever else you need to get going. And of course, the directories for New York, Chicago, and Los Angeles will have the most complete listings, offering you the best possibilities.

GLOSSARY

ARKANSAS TOOTHPICK — For over one hundred years this was another name for the Bowie Knife. Hollywood changed this with the movie ''The Iron Mistress,'' in which a large crude dirk was called an Arkansas Toothpick. Randall soon after introduced a matched set of Bowie and "Toothpick" knives and now everyone recognizes this term to mean a sharp tapered dagger.

BOOT KNIFE — A combat knife with a blade of 3 to 5 inches, meant to be concealed on the person.

BOWIE KNIFE — A large knife with one edge or two, made popular by James Bowie (who died at the Alamo in 1836) but probably designed by his brother, Rezin. The blade may range from 6 to 16 inches. The general idea is an 8- to 10-inch blade with a large clip that is a false edge.

BRASS-WRAPPED TANG — A full tang is reduced in width and covered in brass so that brass shows between the scales instead of steel. Introduced by Bob Loveless.

BUTT — Back end of handle.

BUTT CAP — Metal or other material other than the handle applied at the end, or back, of handle.

CHOIL — Cutaway area between cutting edge and guard.

CLIP — An area on the back of the blade that drops below the straight line in a straight or concave line.

CLIP POINT — The back line breaks sharply and drops to meet the cutting edge.

COCOBOLO — An exotic wood containing enough oil so that it needs no external finish. About two percent of the population is allergic to its dust.

COMBAT KNIFE — Single- or double-edged blade 5 to 10 inches long, double guard.

CONVEX GRIND — Generally a sign of amateur or homemade work. Could be appropriate on a heavy knife meant for chopping.

DROP POINT — A variation of the spear point, in which the point is above the centerline of the blade. Almost always a single-edged hunting knife.

EBONY — A very hard dense wood related to the American persimmon.

ESCUTCHEON — A shield or plate set into the handle to be engraved with the owner's name or initials.

FALSE EDGE — Sharpened back edge of blade (see swedge).

FIGHTING KNIFE — See combat knife.

FINGER GROOVES — Grooves cut into the handle material to make it fit the hand.

FLAT GRIND — Ground flat from edge to back (not hollow ground).

FULL TANG — The tang is the full width of the hand, with two pieces of handle material applied to each side with pins, rivets or screws.

GABOON EBONY — A black or dark brown wood that makes excellent knife handles, except for a tendency to check.

GUARD — The classic term for the cross member affixed to the end of the handle next to the blade. The guard prevents the hand from slipping onto the blade.

HALF TANG — A narrow tang cut to about one-half the length of the handle, usually epoxied into a hole in the handle material, and sometimes also pinned.

HOLLOW GRIND — A cross section of the blade would show it to be concave on both sides. A straight razor is hollow ground.

HUNTING KNIFE — A single-edged blade from 2-1/2 to 6 inches long, with a single guard.

LAMINATED STEEL — A process that apparently developed independently and almost simultaneously in Japan and Scandinavia, in which softer metal is laid on each side of the cutting center core so that it can be left harder.

LINEN MICARTA — Has a cloth reinforcement that is generally cotton, but is **not** linen.

MACCASSER EBONY — A light tan wood with medium to dark brown stripes that makes good handles.

MICARTA — A trademark of Westinghouse which covers phenolic resin reinforced with layers of paper, cloth, wood; available in burgundy, red, green, black, brown, etc. Also available under other names from the manufacturer. Ivory (bone) micarta is not a true micarta; it is an epoxy rather than phenolic.

MORTISED TANG — A combination of the half tang and the scales or handle slabs of the full tang style. The scales are cut out to fit around the half tang and fastened with pins, rivets, or screws. Introduced to modern handmade knives by D.E. Henry.

MOZAMBIQUE EBONY — A black to dark brown member of the rosewood family, not a true ebony. Also called African Blackwood and Grindilla, it is rare but an excellent handle material.

NARROW TANG — The tang portion of the blade runs through a hole in the handle material and is fastened by a nut at the butt or a butt cap.

OBVERSE — That side of a knife seen when you view it with the edge down and the point to your left. This is the side that normally carries the maker's mark.

PLATEN — A steel plate beneath the belt on a belt grinder on which a maker flat grinds a blade or tapers a tang.

POMMEL — Butt area of the blade.

QUILLION — The extension of the guard that is intended to keep the fingers from the blade.

REVERSE — The opposite side from the obverse.

RICASSO — The flat area ahead of the guard that is not included in the principal bevel grinds. The maker's mark is usually in this area.

ROSEWOOD — An exotic wood containing enough oil so that it needs no external finish. Both the East India and the Brazilian rosewoods are suitable for knife handles.

SABER GRIND — A grind having one-fourth to one-half the width of the blade unground.

SCALES — Slabs of handle material applied to a full tang or mortised tang knife. (In pocketknives, these would be called covers and scales would include the liner and bolster.)

SPEAR POINT — Can be single- or double-edged, but is symmetrical in outline. If double-edged, a dagger point is at the centerline of the blade.

STAG — Antler from Europe or India; scales from Sambhar; solid pieces without a porous center from Chital.

STAINLESS STEEL — A steel that has enough nickel or chrome added to discourage oxidation; 440C and 154CM are the two best known that are suitable for knife steels. Stainless steel's bad reputation established prior to 1960 is no longer entirely justified.

SWEDGE — Bevel on the back edge of the blade that is not sharp (see "false edge").

TANG — That portion of the blade that extends into the handle.

TAPERED TANG — The tang is tapered from the guard to the butt, reducing the handle weight. Introduced by Bob Loveless.

UPSWEPT — Generally used to make possible an extreme sweep in the edge. For skinning, the point is above the back line of the blade.